Make Your Own Wooden Kitchen Utensils

Vance Studley

Dover Publications, Inc.

New York

Acknowledgments

I would like to express my gratitude to the following individuals for assisting me with their advice, both editorial and professional, thereby enabling this project to become a reality: Hans Christian Krake for his concise visuals—always artful and clear, his work is deeply appreciated; Susan Mossman for her suggestions and editorial advice; Susan Gies for her careful reading and always helpful comments; Mits Kuwata for remarks on various woods and their use; and Margo Studley, my wife, for hints, ideas, and for being the best of all kitchenmates.

Published in Canada by General Publishing Company, Ltd., 30 Lesmill Road, Don Mills, Toronto, Ontario.

Published in the United Kingdom by Constable and Company, Ltd., 3 The Lanchesters, 162–164 Fulham Palace Road, London W6 9ER.

This Dover edition, first published in 1993, is an unabridged, slightly corrected republication of the work originally published by Van Nostrand Reinhold Company, New York, in 1981.

Manufactured in the United States of America
Dover Publications, Inc., 31 East 2nd Street, Mineola, N.Y. 11501

Library of Congress Cataloging-in-Publication Data

Studley, Vance.
    [Woodworker's book of wooden kitchen utensils]
    Make your own wooden kitchen utensils / Vance Studley.
        p. cm.
    Originally published: Woodworker's book of wooden kitchen utensils. New York : Van Nostrand Reinhold, 1981.
    Includes bibliographical references and index.
    ISBN 0-486-27561-2 (pbk.)
    1. Woodwork. 2. Kitchen utensils.   I. Title.
TT200.S76   1993
674'.88—dc20   92-41040
                                                   CIP

Contents

Introduction

As basic as food itself are the utensils designed and used for its preparation. Cooking, serving, and eating food are time-honored activities that fundamentally involve all of our senses. It follows then that we should be able to gain pleasure from the utensils with which we carry out these activities. Throughout history, man has applied his ingenuity to the creation of a seemingly endless procession of cooking oddities and gadgetry. And why not? The tool is an expression of the very individuality that each good cook brings to his or her own creation. Just as woodworkers, potters, and weavers must come to know the inherent qualities of their materials and their tools, it behooves the cook to know his tools well, for they are the implements with which he exposes the heart of his food.

Providing tools has been a function of the craftsman throughout history, but, today, the designer and maker of the tool are often too far removed from the user. Thus, we are constantly presented with ill-designed objects, shoddy in construction and mass-produced poorly. It has become an unfortunately rare event for us to design and make the tools we need. Faced with the inferiority of many commercially produced items, however, we have come to newly appreciate the forms and qualities of common things crafted and shaped by hand. It is with this thought that I have assembled the projects in this book—thirty-three kitchen utensils, along with step-by-step instructions designed to assist you in arriving at very satisfactory results beginning with the first few efforts.

For the raw material, I have chosen wood as the only, or at least the primary, component. There are several reasons why. Firstly, wood will not impart a flavor to the food. The flavors of many foods are light, subtle, and delicate. Cooking implements that give off metal ions impart a metalic aftertaste, and it is not surprising for people who have a keen, highly developed sense of taste to detect the bitter and unpleasant tincture of metallic essences. Secondly, wood is particularly well suited for food preparation and food serving. Cooks often have personal ways of

making their creations, and wooden tools can be fabricated to meet those special, unique occasions where the usual run-of-the-mill implements fail. Thirdly, the serving and eating of hot food is far more pleasant with wooden utensils. There are no scorchingly hot spoons, ladles, and trivets. Wooden spoons, forks, stirring devices, and the like do not harm metal cookpots, or tear Teflon-coated pans, skillets, or griddles. Wooden bowls, plates, and trays are spared the scratching that accompanies sharp metal against wood.

Last, but not least, is the inherent beauty of the wood itself. It is almost impossible to make an ugly wooden utensil. What's more, wood is sympathetic to the hand and lips and can be fashioned and crafted to the most specific needs.

The inspiration for many of the projects in this book came from parts of the world where true wood cultures evolved and where wood permeated all aspects of daily life. Chief among these is Japan, where, throughout history, aristocrats, townspeople, warriors, and farmers alike have drunk and eaten from wooden bowls and tasted countless dishes prepared with wood and bamboo utensils of intricate and varied shapes.

Many other cultures are sensitive to materials and are extremely fond of wood grains and textures. In Europe, wooden utensils are common, and it is rare to find paints, varnishes, or lacquers on these utensils, since these conceal the surface, practically anathema in the art of using wood. The ravioli cutter of Italy and the Mexican chocolate whipper, called a *molinillo*, might appear unfamiliar to many of us. Yet, these utensils were carefully designed for the preparation of foods common in these countries. I have found alternative uses for many of these unusual items. The molinillo, for instance, makes a delightful honey server.

This book does not intend to be an exhaustive historical study or a complete survey of international cooking implements, nor is it a study of regional cuisines or food itself. I have attempted to include a variety of utensils both simple and complex, to be used

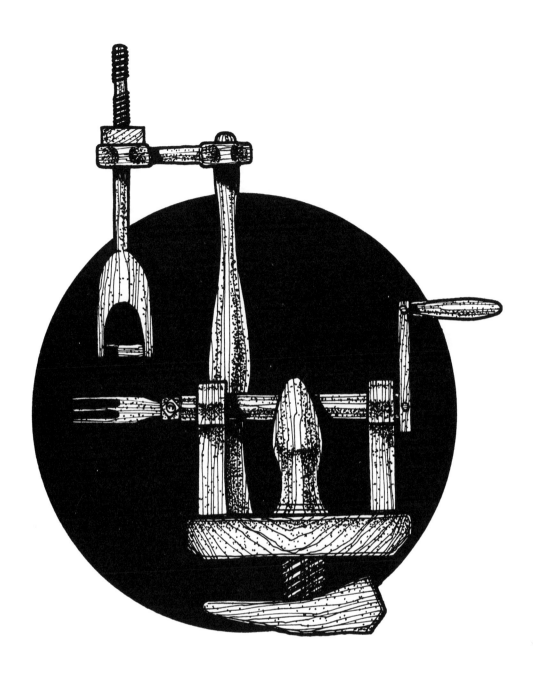

An Early American apple peeler. The homey chore of peeling apples was sheer drudgery to the early American housewife. This ingenious contrivance sped up the routine. An apple was affixed on the fork which was in turn rotated by the cranking handle. An adjustable blade moved across the apple's surface and removed a thin paring. The need to make one's time productive prompted other mechanical gadgets to be invented.

in many different ways. Spoons, ladles, stirrers, strainers, grinders, cutting boards, sieves, paddles, and tongs best fit into this category, and there are spice jars, glass racks, and serving trays, as well. Several utensils can be made within a few hours; others, because of their design, take longer.

Hand tools and a few power-operated tools are all that are required to make any of the projects. If you are a beginning woodworker, start with simple projects (ladles, forks, or a wide-blade spatula) and then work your way up to those projects requiring more advanced techniques. Each utensil has been carefully illustrated to provide you with an overall picture of the item. The working drawings show the dimensions of the utensil and its component pieces.

I would like to encourage you to experiment with different shapes and varieties and to find personal ways to use your creative works to complement your cooking and eating pleasure. After all, food preparation, whether done in the East or West, during the Dark Ages, the Renaissance, or today, consists of the same basic operations—cutting, slicing, mixing, dicing, measuring, forming, and serving. The real advantage to creating your own kitchen utensils is to be able to make decisions about the finished product. To be able to surround yourself with culinary works from your hands, custom-made and tailored for your needs and habits, is as gratifying as the art of making and serving food itself.

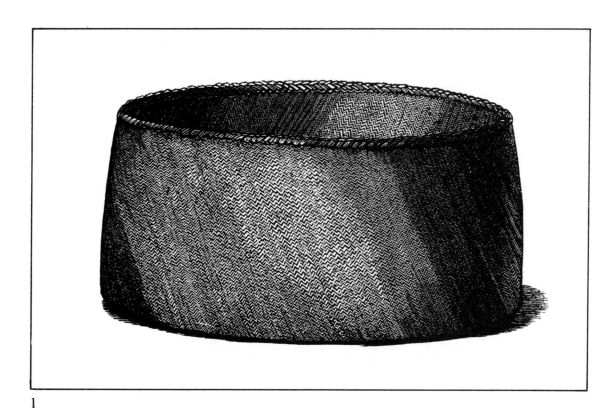

1

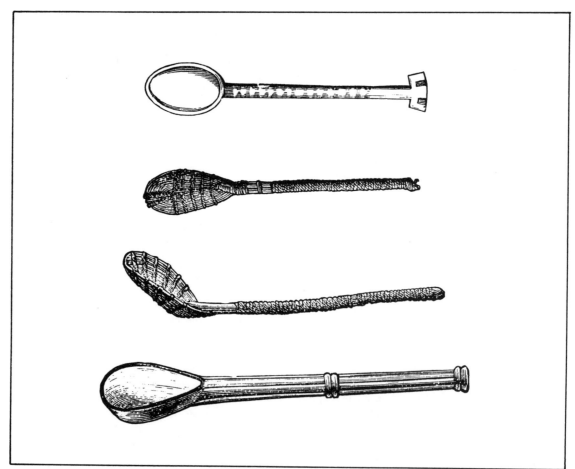

2

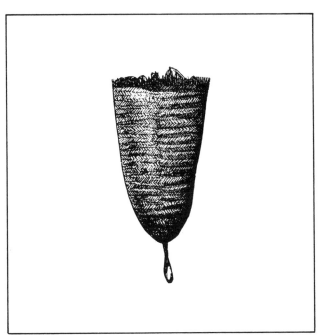

3

In the southern regions of Africa, it is customary for both men and women to participate in the making of cooking implements for the family's use. Shown here are but a few: 1) An African milk basket made entirely of grasses so tightly woven that no leaking is evinced even after several hours of liquid containment. 2) An assortment of African spoons dating back to the 19th century. Again, woven strands of grass were tightly clustered to make stout ladles for milk, water, and other beverages. 3) African bowls, vessels, and baskets created in an impromptu fashion as the need arose. Made of indigenous wood or clay, the vessels evolved in shape over centuries of refined use, but still retained their basic form, enabling the user to tip, carry, and balance the vessel as the occasion saw fit.

1.

The Wood

WHY WOOD?

Somehow, it just seems natural to combine wood with the preparation of food. I know, because I arrived at cooking through the making of wooden utensils; and oddly, as my woodworking efforts improve, so do my culinary achievements.

Wood is a natural material. It exhibits properties that the woodworker embellishes through his shaping and finishing efforts. A craftsman attends to what wood can and cannot do, refusing to make it behave or appear like another material, such as plastic, metal, or glass. Wood does not possess the characteristics that the above-mentioned materials do. Anyone sensitive to wood recoils at the suggestion of masking its unique and special properties. We have all seen examples of wood sprayed with metallic paint to impart a chromelike finish. The result: a form that does a disservice to both polished metal and to wood itself because it becomes, through the painting process, neither of the above. Rather, the woodworker strives to reveal to us what wood is.

One can struggle with wood. Indeed, it is this very quality that accentuates the difference between wood and all other materials and heightens its use. This term "struggle" is not the carpenter's struggle, but the artist's struggle to make it an object that originally was the mind's perception of a form. Wood, in able hands, becomes viable, of service, and has the potential to become very beautiful.

Wood has been in continuous use since man's primordial appearance on earth, and its scarcity has never, until quite recently, been an issue in its use. Exotic woods, such as ebony, padouk, or rosewood, are not as plentiful as pine, fir, or even redwood, but it is this very lack of availability that makes the choice of wood for an anticipated project all the more interesting.

The woods listed in the glossary that follows are a sampling of commonly available commercial woods which are suitable for the projects in this book. I do encourage you, however, to experiment with other varieties that appeal to you as you hunt through your local lumberyard or supplier's shelves.

The "exotic" woods, those which are noted for their excep-tional color, grain, or other properties, would be perfectly acceptable for many of the projects presented here. They are generally more expensive, however, and some are more difficult to work. You might discuss the working properties of any unusual pieces you select with the supplier to be sure of their suitability for the project you have in mind.

I also encourage you to experiment with woods in your locale which may not be available commercially. For example, I have found the wood of citrus trees, such as lemon and orange, to be a lovely pale yellow color, fine textured, and especially nice for carving. Be sure to allow any timber you cut to dry thoroughly before you begin working it.

WOOD GLOSSARY

The following list will give you some idea of the appearance and working properties of many of the commercially available woods.

APPLE

Apple wood is pale, pinkish brown with a fine texture. The grain is often irregular, because the trees tend to be twisted or gnarled. Apple is hard and strong. It is a good choice for carving or turning, but can be difficult to work where the grain is irregular. It can be worked to a nice, smooth finish and stains or polishes very well.

ASH

Ash is pale brown to almost white in color and has a distinctive pattern caused by a band of large pores in each growth ring. Depending on how the wood is cut, these pores can create a pattern of darker lines or wide, irregular bands. Ash is strong and tough. It is one of the few woods which can be steam-bent (Steam-bending is a process whereby the wood is steamed until pliable and then bent to the desired curve or shape. Once dried, the wood will retain this new shape.) Ash is a wood that turns easily and works well.

BAMBOO

Bamboo is actually a treelike grass, the stalks of which are long, hollow tubes marked by joints. Bamboo varies in color and circumference, and the length between joints can be a few inches to a foot or more. A tough, flexible, and versatile material, bamboo can be carved, cut, and otherwise worked with very little finishing required. It must, however, be used only when dry and it must be of a hard composition.

BEECH

Beech wood is a pale, sandy brown and has a fine, even texture and straight grain. Depending on the cut of the wood, the figure or pattern can be fine, smooth parallel lines, or small, darker brown flecks, evenly scattered over the surface. Beech is strong and can be steam-bent or rotary-peeled for veneer. It is a very good turning wood. Beech takes a high polish, and it is particularly good for cooking utensils, because it will not impart any flavor or color to foods.

BIRCH

Birch wood is a very pale yellowish brown, and it has a fine, very uniform texture. In general, it has almost no figure or pattern, but a few varieties, such as "flame" and "masur," do have this feature. It is very heavy, hard, and strong, but it still works and turns well. It will take a fine, smooth finish.

CHERRY

Cherry is a warm, reddish brown with a golden sheen. Fine texture and straight grain are characteristic, and thin brown lines or flecks are often present. Cherry is fairly heavy and strong, and it sometimes has a sweet, roselike scent. It saws easily, works well, and can be finished beautifully by hand or machine.

CHESTNUT

Chestnut wood is pale brown, often with a grayish cast. It has a coarse texture with obvious large pores in each growth ring, which may appear as lines or in broad bands, depending on how the wood is cut. Chestnut is rather light and is not noted for strength, but it is easy to work by hand or machine.

DOUGLAS FIR

The wood is a pale brown, with darker brown markings, which may appear as fine, parallel lines to irregular, wavy bands in a flamelike pattern. It is usually straight grained and may be resinous. It is strong and firm, but has a tendency to splinter. (Quarter-sawn pieces splinter less.) It works well by hand or machine and can take a smooth finish.

ELM

Elm is a pale, sometimes pinkish brown wood with coarse texture. It has a pattern of large and small vessels, which can be seen in irregular bands or lines, and which gives the wood a feathery look (sometimes called "partridge-breast" figuring). Occasional pieces are highly figured with swirls of light and dark in a beautiful pattern. These pieces come from irregular growth on the tree called "burls." There are several different species of elm

available, and, of these, rock and wych elm are the hardest and strongest. The irregular grain makes the elm almost impossible to split, but it works well, turns fairly well, and bends well. An important feature of elm is its ability to hold up in the water-logged state; therefore, it would be an ideal choice for a utensil which will be in frequent or constant use with fluids.

HICKORY

Hickory ranges from white to red-brown, depending upon the part of the tree from which the timber comes. The white sapwood is generally superior. It is straight grained and coarse textured, and it is hard, heavy, and stiff. Hickory has the ability to withstand sudden pressure, which explains its use in tool handles and athletic equipment. The wood is sometimes difficult to work, especially if knotty or irregularly grained. Hickory has a very unique scent when burned and is used for smoking foods. If used for a cooking utensil, it might impart a flavor or odor to the food.

HOLLY

Holly is a white to grayish wood with a fine, even texture. The general appearance of the wood is quite plain, but the grain is often irregular. It is heavy and hard, and it is not very stable in damp conditions. It is difficult to work by hand, but machines well, and takes stains very nicely.

LINDEN

Also known as basswood, linden is a very pale yellowish or buff-colored wood with straight grain and a very fine, even texture. It has no figure or pattern. Somewhat soft and light, it is not a strong wood, but it works easily and turns well. It is a good choice for carving and can be stained with ease.

MAHOGANY

Mahogany is a medium-textured, reddish brown wood, generally categorized as either African or American. Though the two are quite similar in color and both are fairly light in weight, some have dark flecks or thin lines. Mahogany saws easily and can be worked to a fine, smooth finish.

MAPLE

There are many varieties of maple, but all have similar pale reddish-brown color. (Sugar and black maples are somewhat heavier, harder, and stronger than other maples.) Maple is fairly heavy, strong, and hard, with good shock resistance. It has straight grain, and sugar maple occasionally produces a lovely, "bird's-eye" figure of tiny dark spots. When found, such pieces are regularly used for veneer, so blocks or pieces of figured wood are rare. Maple is an excellent wood for carving or turning. It finishes nicely and wears slowly.

OAK

Both red and white oak are available commercially, with white being superior in most respects. Red oak is more pinkish, and the figuring is less pronounced. It is also somewhat harder to work than white oak, but it can still yield a most acceptable product.

White oak is nearly white to a pale yellow-brown in color. It has a coarse texture, with very evident large pores. The grain is usually straight, and the figure in the wood is created by the growth rings and rays. It may appear as a series of lines, or, on quarter-sawn surfaces, as broad bands of harder, denser wood, which clearly reflects the light. This unique feature is referred to as "silver grain" and is a primary reason for oak's popularity as a furniture wood. Oak is heavy, strong, dense, and almost waterproof. It can be hard to work, because of this combination of properties, and can be finished very nicely. Wooden pegs are often used to join oak, because some metals (especially iron) will react with the tannins in the wood, causing dark, inklike stains.

OLIVE

Olive is a particularly attractive pale brown wood with dark brown or gray markings in a marblelike pattern. The texture is fine and the grain is often irregular. It is a good choice for turning or carving, and, though hard to saw, it can be worked well by hand or machine. Olive finishes very nicely, providing a fine, smooth surface, which stains and polishes well.

PINE

There are a great variety of pines available as commercial timber. The color varies from pale yellow-brown to red-brown, sometimes with darker markings, depending on the species. The wood, in general, is medium- to coarse textured, straight grained, moderately strong, and quite easy to work. Some pines are knotty, and the irregularities in the grain must be handled more carefully. Resin may occasionally build up on tools, and the wood often gives off a turpentinelike odor when worked. Pine wears well and can be finished nicely.

WALNUT

Walnut is a beautifully figured wood, usually a grayish-brown, with black streaks or wavy bands. It is a medium-textured wood, with straight grain, and it is heavy, strong, and hard. Walnut carves well and takes stains readily.

American black walnut has working properties similar to other walnuts, but in different color. It is generally darker chocolate to purple-brown, with very dark streaks or lines, and the texture is coarser. Black walnut has a distinctive odor and even taste, and this should be considered when making a utensil that will come in direct contact with foods.

WILLOW

Willow wood is grayish to reddish brown, with some darker lines or streaks. It has a fine, even texture and is a soft, low-strength wood. It works easily and resists splintering. It can be finished nicely and is often used for artificial limbs, because it is light, but tough.

THE USE AND CARE OF WOOD

Wood has long been part of the kitchen mystique. Just picture a chef, and, most likely, you envision him wielding a wooden spoon or rolling pin. Butcher blocks, carving boards, and salad bowls are common, but they are only the beginning—a trifling sample of the vast array of cooking paraphernalia that can be made of wood.

Quite simply, wood is an ideal medium for kitchen utensils. It is noiseless, conspicuously without the clink, clatter, and scrape of its metal counterparts. Wood is infinitely more durable in many instances than other materials. It doesn't scratch, needs no polishing, nor does it melt like plastics. With care, your wooden utensils will last for many years and will age gracefully.

It must be remembered, though, that wood is not indestructible and continued use is bound to leave its mark. Washings and repeated heavy-duty use will certainly affect your wooden utensils, so it is important to follow a few safety measures. With proper care, the wood *will* age, but gracefully and with character.

When using and cleaning your utensils, simply keeping in mind the nature of wood itself and using a little common sense will go a long way toward keeping them in good shape. For example, a porous, unfinished wood left to soak in a liquid for any length of time will, obviously, absorb some of the liquid. A wooden handle resting on the edge of a hot pan will eventually scorch. Wood will discolor, burn, swell, dry, splinter, or crack, if abused.

You will find endless uses for your wooden trays, platters, servers, spoons, and such, but do give special attention to wood surfaces that come into contact with raw meats and highly seasoned foods. Use hard, finely textured woods, which will stand up to chopping and pounding and which will absorb juices less readily for these purposes. Oak is a good choice for cutting boards; beech is excellent for use with oily foods and substances, because it resists fatty residues and cleans easily.

Clean your wooden utensils in warm, soapy water immediately after use, whenever possible. If the surface has become grooved over time, use a brush to remove particles and juices from the crevices. Rinse thoroughly and allow to dry at room temperature.

After preparing highly seasoned or flavored ingredients, such as garlic, onions, or peppers, wash the utensils before using them again to prepare other foods. Otherwise, you will transfer the flavors or odors from one food to another. Also, raw meat juices, raw eggs, and milk products can spoil and become harmful. Be sure to clean your tools immediately and thoroughly when preparing such items.

At the stove, you'll find wooden tools wonderfully sympathetic to cooking activities. What could be gentler to an omelette than a wooden rice paddle? Soup, served up by a generous ladle, has a special warmth. But, here, too, care should be taken to protect your handmade ware. Do not leave utensils sitting in hot oil or long-simmering liquids. Use a spoon rest (of your own design?) to keep tools handy, but avoid the possibility of scorching the wood or having it absorb undue moisture from the cooking pot.

Do not use your wooden ware in an oven, except, occasionally perhaps to keep a dish warm for a brief time before serving. Prolonged exposure to the heat of the oven will dry the wood. The same is true of the refrigerator. Placing a dish of condiments in the refrigerator for a while before serving won't do any damage, but a long stay in a self-defrosting refrigerator will dehydrate the wood, just as it will unprotected food.

Fortunately, the microwave oven is much kinder to wood. In fact, a wooden bowl, tray, or platter is ideal for warming or reheating foods in the microwave. Prolonged cooking or high settings are not recommended, as these procedures will dry the wood and possibly cause cracking. I suggest you consult your microwave manufacturer's instructions for the proper settings. Any wooden stirring utensil can be left in the microwave for short periods to facilitate mixing or moving the food during the course of the cooking. Bread, warmed on its own serving board, or individual casseroles on their own trivets can go directly to the table.

Again, the best cleaning procedure is to wash your tools in warm, soapy water, rinse thoroughly, and dry. Avoid prolonged soaking in the wash or rinse water. Wood can be placed in the dishwasher, but watch for signs of dryness from the heat and detergent and be sure to reseason the piece with oil (see finishing instructions in Chapter 3) when necessary.

For food stains on wood with an oil finish, a solution of warm water and a small amount of detergent with sulfur (one-half teaspoon detergent to one pint of water) can be used. Dip a clean cloth in the solution, wring out, and rub over the stained area. Deep or stubborn stains may not be completely removed by this method. For such extreme cases, or if splintering or rough edges has occurred, resanding and reseasoning the tool is suggested.

Of course, change in color and signs of wear should be expected. As with all good tools, these will take on the rich patina of time. Use them, enjoy them, and let them inspire you to new efforts in the kitchen and at the workbench.

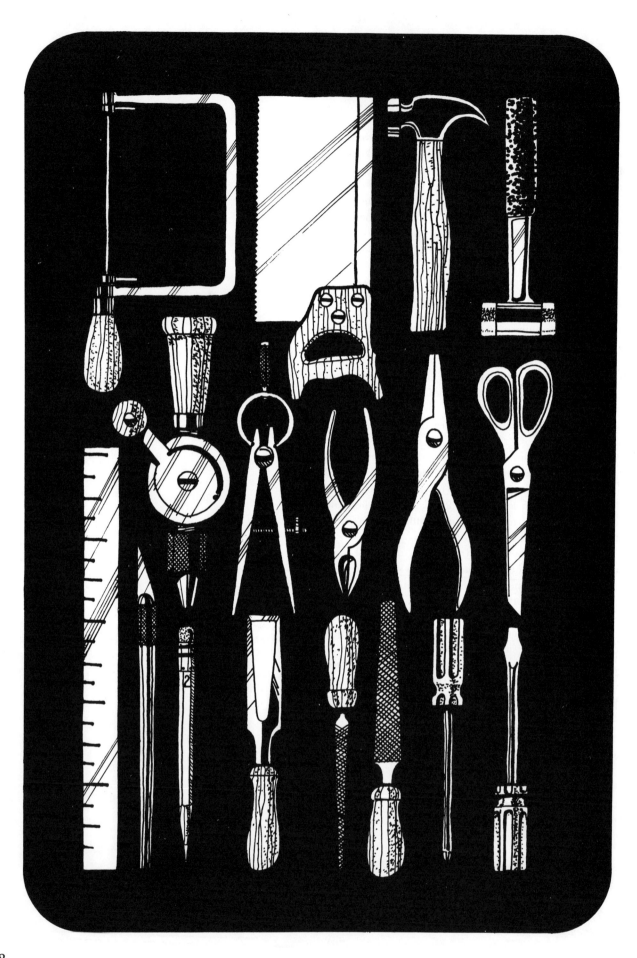

12

2.

The Equipment

THE TOOLS AND ACCESSORIES

The kinds of tools and materials used in the design and making of wooden kitchen utensils vary with the extent to which the woodworker intends to carry his work. There exists in this book a large number of simple utensils and implements, which can be constructed with limited equipment. Indeed, the majority of tools required for any of the projects fall well within the range of tools the beginner is likely to have within the home workshop. Improvisation can take the person new to woodworking a long way toward accomplishing results within his limitations. Clamps, hammers, pliers, and files need not be sophisticated and costly, but they should be sound in construction and in good working order. A rusty coping saw blade or a loose-fitting hammer head does more to impede progress than would the temporary absence of the tool while you set about to mend it and restore it to useful condition. Lack of expensive woodworking equipment, such as power lathes and drills, overcomplicated table saws, and disk sanders need not prevent anyone from experiencing the pleasure of making cookware and kitchen utensils.

A list of tools and materials commonly used in the making of wooden cooking utensils follows, with a brief description of each. Historically, many of the items featured in the following pages were conceived in a time when tools like the ones we're used to using today were nonexistent. Crude axes, dull jack planes, augers, and bits were the workman's tools of the trade, and remarkably ingenious contrivances and gadgets often resulted by the measure of a man's hands and not necessarily by a steel tape measure and space-age micrometers. Therefore, if you are a se-

The woodworker's assortment of hand tools to be used in the design and making of small food utensils. There is little that is exotic or difficult to obtain in this assortment of inexpensive tools. The utensil maker need not feel inhibited for lack of sophisticated machinery.

rious craftsman, take advantage of the items provided in the tool list. Add to your toolbox as the occasion arises, and, in the meantime, take pleasure in starting off with simple means and realistic objectives. Soon, your kitchen will be transformed into another kind of enjoyable workspace, radiant with wooden spoons, trays, racks, spice bottles, water ladles, balloon whisks, and a whole host of useful and very handsome implements.

RULES AND SQUARES

There are a great number of tools for measuring and marking stock and determining angles. For the purpose of this book, only a tape measure and try square are essential.

A good retractable **tape measure** has a flexible steel tape with a sturdy hook attachment on the leading end. The flexible tape allows for measuring circumferences and angles, as well as straight surfaces. One with metric indications on one edge might be advisable.

The **try square** is an L-shaped tool with a steel blade set at a right (90-degree) angle to a wooden handle. Try squares are used for marking stock for square or parallel cuts, truing corners, etc. The most reliable try squares are composed of an L-shaped piece of steel, one end of which becomes the blade, while the other end, fitted with wood on each side, is the handle. This eliminates the possibility of the joint becoming loose and inaccurate over time.

DIVIDERS AND CALIPERS

Dividers and calipers are tools used to measure or transfer measurements from one piece to another, from rule or pattern to stock, etc. They come in a variety of shapes and sizes and are characterized by two "legs" attached at one end with a movable joint.

The **outside caliper** is used for measuring outside dimensions. It has legs, which curve outward from the joint and then in toward each other at the tips. For the projects in this book, outside calipers will be more useful than **inside calipers**. (These have straight legs with tips pointing outward and are used for interior measuring).

Calipers are helpful in measuring and marking the inner and outer diameter of boxes, jars, and other utensils designed to be self-enclosed. Dimensioning is matched with a tape measure or a straight ruler. Calipers are available in retail hardware stores.

Dividers have generally straight legs and taper to points on each tip. They can be used for transfering measurements or for checking measurements as work progresses.

VISES AND CLAMPS

Vises and clamps are used for holding stock in position, either while it is being worked with tools, or while glue or adhesive is drying. A good table vise is the most convenient for most clamping procedures, but a set of C-clamps or wood clamps can be used with blocks of hardwood to hold stock securely on the work surface. Clamps are especially good for exerting pressure during drying processes.

Mounted on the workbench, a **woodworker's vise** has two movable jaws, which should be lined with ¾-inch hardwood blocks to protect the stock from marks and dents. The stock is placed between the jaws and the vise is tightened until the piece is held firmly in place. It should not be overtightened, as this is likely to mark the stock and puts undue pressure on the jaws.

The **C-clamp** is a very versatile tool, shaped like a C, with a large screw and shoe running through one end for tightening the clamp over the work. C-clamps are available in a variety of sizes from ¾ to 12 inches. One or two pairs in different sizes are handy for a variety of uses. It is a good idea to place a thin piece of wood between the clamp and the stock to protect the surface from scars and marks.

HAND SCREWS

Wooden hand screws are ideal for clamping on an angle or for nonparallel pieces. They consist of two pieces of hardwood, held together by two large bolts, which can be adjusted separately to accommodate different angles.

SAWS

Saws are used for cutting and dimensioning wood. Handsaws are available in a variety of shapes and sizes and are used for different purposes. The most important distinction among saws is in the arrangement and formation of the teethcross-cut saws designed for cutting across the grain and rip saws designed for cutting with the grain of the wood.

Generally for cutting smaller pieces of stock or joints, the **backsaw** has a rectangular blade. A heavy steel strip runs along the top edge of the blade for support. Backsaws most commonly have cross-cut teeth for working across the grain, but they are available with fine rip-saw teeth, for special needs where cutting with the grain is required.

Coping saws have a C-shaped frame and replaceable thin blades, which are held under tension by adjustable pins at either end of the frame. The blade can be angled to cut in any direction, making the saw very useful for cutting irregular shapes, curves, etc.

Designed to cut across the grain, the **cross-cut saw** has a long, tapering blade with teeth facing alternately to each side. A larger-toothed saw is best for rough cuts and softer woods. A saw with finer, more numerous teeth is better for hardwoods and more detailed work.

Hacksaws are used to cut metal. They have a bowlike frame and interchangeable blades, the frame often being adjustable to accommodate blades of various lengths. Those with a pistol-grip handle are generally more comfortable to work with.

HAMMERS AND MALLETS

Hammers are used for pounding and come in shapes and sizes to suit various needs. A good-quality hammer is a must for any woodworker, and, for the purposes of this book, a soft-faced mallet will also be required.

The standard carpenter's hammer, called **claw hammer**, has a tapered and curved split "claw" opposite the head, which is used for removing nails. A steel shaft permanently affixed to the head makes for the most reliable tool, preventing the loosening of the joint with continued use.

The **soft-faced mallet** is used when a standard hammer would be likely to mar the surface or for driving carving tools. The head of the mallet is made of rubber or coiled rawhide, which is gentle to the wood, yet provides a firm blow when necessary.

The **wood or carver's mallet** is a heavy mallet used in carving to drive the chisel. The wood mallet has a head of lignum vitae or, sometimes, beech. It has a round, cork-shaped head, which makes it convenient for use at various angles.

SCREWDRIVERS

A tool used for driving or turning screws into or out of the stock. Several different tip configurations and sizes are available, but the most commonly used are flared-tip and Phillips. To avoid damaging either the screw or the stock, use a screwdriver which fits firmly into the screw head and is the right size.

Flared-tip screwdrivers are used to drive screws with a single slot. It is helpful to have several in varying widths to accommodate screws of different sizes. Sets are available with a single handle and interchangeable shafts with different-sized tips.

The **Phillips screwdriver** is for use with Phillips-head screws, which have a cross-shaped slot, slightly rounded on the interior angles. The screwdriver tip has four flutes, each tapering to a point.

PLIERS

Pliers are gripping tools used to position and hold stock or hardware in place. There are a great many styles available. For our purposes, a slip-joint pliers and a needle-nosed, or snipe-nosed, are all that is required.

The jaws of the **slip-joint pliers** are blunt tipped, with a flat and a curved gripping surface, both marked with fine serrations. The slip joint allows you to adjust the pliers for two different widths.

Designed for small objects or small spaces, **snipe-nosed (or**

Hammers designed for specific duties. These offer the wood-worker a choice when it comes time to delicately tap a wooden dowel or to give a mighty whack in nailing boxes. From top to bottom are a high-impact plastic-headed mallet, a claw hammer for general woodworking operations, a tacking hammer used to tap small brads, and a ballpeen hammer used to round out metalic materials.

needle-nosed) pliers have long, tapering jaws, which come to a point at the end. Fine serrations line the jaws and the handles are bowed outward to fit comfortably between palm and fingers.

The **channel lock or waterpump pliers** has the same kind of joint as the slip-joint variety, but with more positions or width adjustments available. The jaws of the tool are at an angle to the handles, which are longer than those on the slip-joint pliers. Though often used in plumbing, these are sometimes most convenient for holding round stock or stock placed in an unusual position.

JACK PLANE

The jack plane is 14 to 15 inches long and has a cutting iron width of 2 inches. It is used for dimensioning wood, shaving off peelings to quickly reduce high spots, or for removing small amounts of wood where cutting is impractical. The cutting iron runs along the bottom of the tool and can be adjusted. The top portion has two handles, a grip in the rear and a knob in the front for comfortable handling.

DRILLS AND BRACES

Drills and braces are used for boring holes. Both kinds of tools are available with interchangeable bits.

The **brace** turns the bit by the rotation of the frame which is curved outward in a C shape between the chuck and head. The brace provides for continuous rotation of the bit, instead of the stop-and-go action of simple drills and augers, where the hand must be repositioned after each turn. A rachet attached to the chuck will facilitate use where there is not room for a complete rotation of the handle.

Among the bits available for the brace, the **auger bits** are good choices for drilling holes in wood. Auger bits range from ¼ to 1½ inches in diameter and have helical twists, which continue up the shank, clearing the waste out of the hole as it is bored. The double twist, or Jennings, bit has a double helical twist. The single twist, or solid center, bit is the strongest and best configuration for very long bits. Auger bits are more easily kept centered in deep holes than the center bit.

The common **hand drill** is equipped with a gear ratio and is hand-driven by means of a rotating handle. The chuck will hold drill bits from 1/64 to ½ inch in diameter. This type of drill is often used to make holes for starting screws, etc., but it may also be used to drill metal if a lubricant is used.

A selection of standard twist or Morse **drill bits** is useful, especially if the hand drill is used extensively. Dowel bits are designed for drilling in end or side grains and have two spurs in addition to a center point to help keep the drill from wandering off center.

AWLS

Awls are used for piercing or starting holes for nails, screws, etc. The **straight awl** has a wooden, knoblike handle with a straight, cylindrical shaft, tapering to a sharp point. For most drilling procedures, it is advisable to mark the starting point or center of the intended hole with the awl, and then position the point of the drill bit in the indentation to assure proper alignment.

RASPS AND FILES

These tools are used for smoothing wood, enlarging holes, or removing burrs and rough spots. In general, rasps are rougher and remove wood more quickly than files. Both come in a variety of shapes and textures. Those listed below are some of the more common ones and those most suited to the projects included in this book.

Files come in several varieties and range from coarse to fine. Single-cut files have parallel rows of teeth, and double-cut files have a second set of parallel rows cut at a 45-degree angle to the first set. Double-cut files are for rough work, single-cut for more delicate operations. Both single and double-cut files can range from coarse (**bastard**), to medium, to fine, depending on the number and placement of the teeth. The shape of the file may be **flat** (with two flat working surfaces), **half-round** (with a curved surface and a flat surface), and **round** (a cylindrical, tapering file for curved surfaces and enlarging holes). **Needle or jeweler's files** are very small and delicate and are used for detailed work.

Rasps are used for quick wood removal and they also come in coarse or fine varieties. The most common wood rasp is shaped like a half-round file, though there are also flat and round rasps available. The rasp teeth vary from file teeth by being individually formed to cut away small slivers of wood.

The **Surform files (round and flat)** are unique in that the blades are made of perforated steel. The sharp edges of the perforations cut the wood, and the waste passes through the holes and away from the work surface. Another advantage of Surform files is that the blades are removable from the frame and can be replaced. They can be used for the same purposes as the rasp.

CHISELS AND GOUGES

Chisels and gouges are used for shaping and carving wood or making small cuts. They can be used by hand alone or with a soft-faced mallet to drive them.

The **chisel** has a flat, rectangular blade with a cutting edge on the end. Commonly available in widths from ⅛ to ¾ inch, chisels are often purchased in sets of commonly used sizes.

Gouges are similar to chisels, but the blade is curved in cross section, with the cutting bevel being either on the outer or the inner edge of the curve. Common blade widths range from ¼ to 1 inch.

POWER TOOLS

Though the projects in this book are designed for those who have even just a modest workshop equipped with basic hand tools, some power tools are convenient for accomplishing the work more quickly and easily. Below are the power tools most applicable for our purposes.

The **saber saw** is a hand-held power saw. It can accomplish a number of cutting jobs, but is not designed for cutting very large or thick sections of lumber. There are a number of special blades for cutting different materials, such as metal and plaster, as well as coarse and fine blades for wood. The saber saw is a very versatile tool and is good for cutting irregular shapes or whenever extensive cutting by hand is required.

The **bench jigsaw** is ideal for those jobs which require intricate cuts or tight curves, since it leaves both hands free to guide the stock through the saw. Saber saw blades may be used in some jigsaws, but a jeweler's blade is specially designed for it. Sanding and file attachments are available for some models.

If the woodworker could have only one power tool in his shop, perhaps the best choice would be the **hand or power drill**. With its many attachments, it can do many tasks. A variable speed drill offers the woodworker much more versatility and a reverse switch allows for the removal of screws. Hole saws, screwdriver bits, countersink bits, and sanding disks are among the most popular attachments.

The **drill press** is a more sophisticated and accurate drill, appropriate for large-scale projects or exacting work. The stock is positioned to the fixed table, and the drill, positioned above the table, is lowered by a feed level, bringing the bit into contact with the stock. A drill press is especially useful for drilling metals.

The **belt sander** is used to remove wood quickly, by means of a continuously moving belt, traveling around rollers on the underside of the machine. The sander can be used across the grain (to remove material quickly) or with the grain for a finer finish. Various kinds and grits of abrasive paper come in belt form for use with the belt sander.

As the name implies, the **disk sander** works by means of a revolving disk, sanding in a circular motion. The disk section can be of rubber or metal and supports the abrasive paper circles, which do the sanding. The disk sander will leave scratches on the wood surface, so it should be used only for the roughest sanding operations. A disk sanding attachment can be used with the power drill, and abrasive papers are also available in various textures and substances.

SANDPAPERS

Although not actually made of sand anymore, abrasive papers still carry the general name of sandpaper. They are available in a wide variety of materials and textures to suit specific needs. Abrasives are categorized as coarse, medium, and fine, with subdivisions in each category. Some have the particles arranged close together (closed coat), and these cut quickly, but clog easily. Papers with the grain more widely dispersed (open coat) clog less readily and are best for removing paint or finishes.

They are numbered to indicate the degree of coarseness, the lower the number, the coarser the paper. For the projects in this book, a supply of four grades—120, 220, 280, and 400—will be adequate. The various kinds of abrasives are described here.

Flint or glasspaper is the cheapest abrasive, but one which wears quickly. It can be used for rough finishing, but is not recommended for fine work.

Garnet paper is naturally red and is a familiar abrasive. It is harder than flint and available in finer grades. It would be used dry.

Usually used for sanding metal, **emery paper** is available with paper or cloth backing and can be used wet or dry.

Harder than emery paper, **synthetic silicon carbide**, which is a synthetic paper, is waterproof, so it can be used with water on metal. For use on wood, it should be kept dry.

Aluminum oxide is available with paper or cloth backing. Aluminum is another synthetic abrasive, which can be used on wood and is often used when machine sanding.

THE WORK SPACE

Ideally, the work space should be a well-lit, open environment where an occasional spill will not cause concern. The scale of the majority of the utensils covered in this book does not require an extensive woodworking shop or even a special place in which only crafts are to be carried out. Very few of the materials are even remotely toxic. (Solvents, sealers, finishes, etc. that are toxic have been kept to an extreme minimum.) Eating and serving utensils are not designed to have toxic ingredients as part of their composition.

A sturdy and well-built **worktable** is a must. Clamping, sawing, sanding and similar procedures are carried out on this table, and a flimsy table does little to help the woodworker in his creative efforts.

An inexpensive **goose-neck lamp** fitted with a 100-watt bulb can be installed on the table allowing flexibility in illumination. Sanding is best done outdoors or near an open window.

A large roll of **Kraft paper or butcher's wrap** makes an ideal table covering to be disposed of after a work session.

A simple **pegboard outfitted** with hand tools puts the woodworker's tools in full view. This is for those moments when the search for a misplaced screwdriver would cost assembly time that could best be spent in more productive ways.

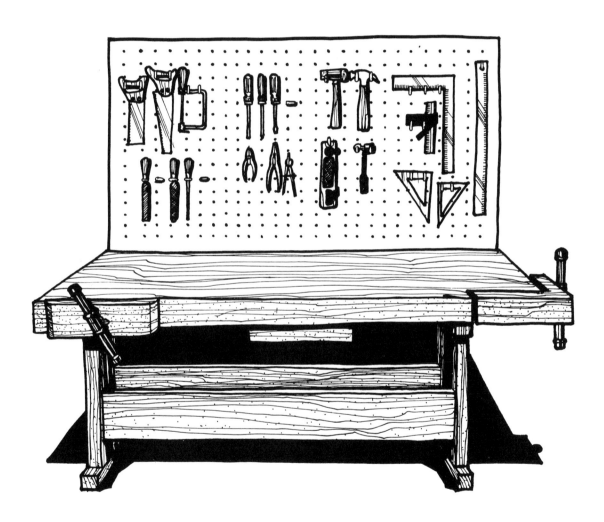

The workbench must be sturdy and able to withstand punishment meted out by saws, hammers, drills, and assembly procedures, all of which are inherent in the utensil-making process. A simple pegboard mounted to the wall puts tools on display for easy access.

3.

The Work

ABOUT THE PROJECTS

The projects in the next five chapters range from the very simple to the more complex. If you are a novice, work on the simpler projects first, such as spatulas, spoons, and ladles. Later, once you've mastered some of the basics, work up to the more challenging ones.

Your first attempts should closely follow the instructions to give best results. Consider changing scale, for example, only after you have made the utensil once to familiarize yourself with the basic configurations and procedures set forth.

As you make the projects in the book, you will find that modification here and a variation there might make the tool perfect for another use. Or, you might pick up a piece of wood that suggests a new form or shape to you. Because wood and food go so nicely together, you may be inspired by a certain recipe or technique to create an implement or serving piece just as unique—a spoon with just the right curve to the bowl, a scoop that holds a commonly needed measure, a plank the perfect size for your favorite steak. Take your mental notes to the wood shop and translate them into reality. Ask family and friends for ideas too, and visit specialty shops for inspiration. You'll soon have more ideas than you can find time for.

Once you have your project in mind, the next step is to choose the wood. The section on woods in this book will be of help to you, and, of course, availability and your own personal likes and dislikes will play a major role in your choice. With that important decision settled, you are ready to begin the work.

MAKING THE PATTERNS

The first step in construction is to transfer the measurements or pattern to the stock. For simple shapes, measuring and marking can be done directly on the wood itself. For example, if the project calls for a 4- by 4-inch piece of ½-inch stock, inspect the wood for the best cutting area (a solid, smooth place free from unwanted knots, etc., but which will not produce unnecessary waste), and

then mark out a 4- by 4-inch block. Use a square to be sure the corners are true. Then proceed with the cutting.

For more complex pieces, it is wise to make a paper pattern of the exact size and dimensions, and then trace or transfer it to the stock. To make a pattern for any of the projects given in the book, you might use one of the following methods. Regardless of which method you use be sure to make a pattern for each side of the utensil that will require guidelines for cutting or carving (i.e., top, bottom, right, left, face, back).

GRID METHOD

Trace the drawing of the utensil, using a piece of tracing paper and a dark pencil or marker. Next, draw a grid pattern over the tracing, using the measurements given on the drawing as the basis for the size of your grid squares. For example, if a spoon's length is given as 12 inches, divide the area into twelve equal areas (even though the drawing may be only 6 inches long). The distance between each of your lines will represent 1 inch. Draw a set of lines at right angles to the first set and the same distance apart.

The next step is to draw a new grid on a piece of clean paper with the spaces measuring the actual 1 inch. Now, transfer the drawing of the spoon to the larger grid by marking on it with a dot wherever the outline of the traced spoon intersects the smaller grid. This will give you a series of dots on the larger grid which, when connected, will be the enlarged outline of the spoon.

This same procedure can be used to enlarge or reduce the pattern to any desired size, simply by drawing the appropriately sized grid over your tracing and proceeding from there.

OPAQUE PROJECTOR METHOD

An opaque or overhead projector can be very useful for enlarging or reducing drawings of all kinds. Opaque projectors can often be rented from camera or art-supply stores, and some public libraries or schools have then available for a small fee.

To enlarge a drawing from the book simply put the open book in the appropriate place, and adjust the projector until the projected image is the size you want. Then, trace the image on a clean sheet of paper.

TRANSFERRING THE PATTERNS

To transfer the pattern to the stock you may cut out the pattern, place it on the stock, and trace around it with a soft pencil or scribing tool. If you plan to do this, be sure to use a heavy paper for your pattern pieces. Another way to transfer the markings is with carbon paper, placing it between the pattern and the stock. To make your own "carbon," turn the pattern paper over, and, using a soft pencil or a piece of charcoal, rub back and forth across the area to be traced. Turn the paper right side up, and position it on the stock. Draw firmly around the shape on your original line, and the graphite or charcoal on the back will transfer to the wood. Now you are ready to cut.

WORKING THE PROJECTS: CLUES AND SUGGESTIONS

Woodworking in general can be facilitated by using good wood that has been carefully examined and prepared. This means avoid warped pieces, damp woods, or woods showing evidence of cracks, fissures, or knots even though a lower price is its attractive feature.

Tools must be properly maintained. Teeth on saws are to be sharp. Edges of knives, gouges, and chisels are to be finely honed, and clamps are to be manipulated with ease. Oil hand tools or power equipment, if indicated, and clean working parts according to manufacturer's instructions.

Never discard usable scraps regardless of size. They will come in handy for some future, yet undefined, project and can often be used as accent pieces of for small inlay work. Exotic woods should be identified with marking pen and masking tape.

Avoid any toxic substances in cases where food will come into contact with the wood's surface. Manufacturers' labels are required to state whether toxic substances are contained in glues, adhesives, solvents, finishes and the like. Don't trust any unmarked substance to be safe.

Clamping is required whenever moving blades, parts, drill bits, and machinery are used. The few minutes saved in sidestepping a clamping step are not worth the gamble. Use a push stick if you cut wood on a bandsaw, table saw or radial arm saw.

Dust is the enemy of the woodworker who is in the process of finishing his or her project with a liquid substance. Always perform this operation in a dust-free environment.

Save small glass and metal jars to be used for storage of nails, pins, screws, brads, grommets, hinges, washers, brads, and a hundred other small items that are easily misplaced and that tend to clutter the work bench.

Working the projects is a step-by-step affair. Rehearse your steps before you actually begin and think through each operation in what you consider to be the best sequence of events. Although every attempt has been made to help you prepare yourself and your work area for each project, perhaps your own particular working methods will work best for you. Your working style is perhaps not altogether that different from many other woodworkers and the one attribute common to all good craftsmen is organization before and while the project is underway.

FINISHING UP

In most woodworking projects, a good amount of time and energy must be devoted to the finishing process. After careful sanding is completed and the item has been cleaned to remove dust and sanding residue, any number of stains, fillers, and/or sealers may be applied to the wood to enhance and protect it.

As with wood selection, the process of choosing a finish is a personal, as well as practical, consideration. The degree of shine, change in color, and the hardness and permanence of the finishing material must all be weighed and a choice made so as to complete the project with just the right touch.

In the selection of finishes for cooking utensils, the process is somewhat simplified. First of all, the natural look, feel, and the quality of wood lend themselves beautifully to the atmosphere of the kitchen and dining area. But important too is the fact that any item that comes into contact with food should be kept safe, clean, and nontoxic. Since the tough, transparent finishing materials, like varnish or lacquer, most often used on wood will eventually wear away with continued use, they are not recommended for any item that will be used directly in the preparation or serving of food.

Where wood is used for purposes other than the direct manipulation of the foodstuffs, the woodworker may choose to use such a finishing material, without worry of its coming into repeated contact with the food. For a handle, trivet, or rack, if a hard, permanent finish is desired, varnish, penetrating oil, or lacquer finishes are suggested. Read and follow manufacturer's instructions carefully. When choosing such a finish, be sure to check the product's resistance to heat and moisture, if the piece is likely to come into contact with either or both.

The majority of projects in this book, if not all, would be nicely handled with as simple a finish as possible. The only reason for using any preparation at all is to lubricate and replenish the natural oils of the wood, which are depleted by constant washing or subjection to heat and moisture. For those items actually used in food preparation, I would recommend rubbing them with a little oil to season them and repeating the process occasionally to restore their beauty and suppleness.

The procedure is as follows: for the initial oiling, clean the wood thoroughly of dust and sanding residue by wiping it with a clean, soft cloth or tack rag. Then, use a small amount of oil (mineral oil is harmless and will not turn rancid, but vegetable oils or olive oil may be used for pieces that will be washed regularly), and apply it to the wood with a piece of soft cloth. Rub the oil into the wood with the cloth or with your hand, first going across the grain and then with the grain to work it into the surface. Warming the oil slightly will help it to penetrate. If you are working on a larger item, do one area at a time, rubbing the oil in thoroughly and then moving on. After the oil has been applied, wipe the entire piece with a clean, soft cloth, rubbing gently to remove any excess oil which has remained on the surface. Allow the piece to rest overnight, and repeat the oiling process. If the wood appears dry in certain places, you can repeat immediately, until an even overall appearance is achieved.

Use your own judgment to decide when to give the utensil additional treatments. Remember that as it is used, oil from the hands acts to lubricate the handle portion, and fats and oils from cooking may penetrate the working end of the tool. But, repeated washing can remove natural oils from the wood, too.

DISPLAYING THE PROJECTS

Part of the enjoyment of good food comes in its presentation. So, too, displaying the tools of the cooking craft adds special appeal to the kitchen and sparks the imagination of the cook. The tools presented here are functional—some are designed for quite specific tasks and others serve an abundance of uses. But, they are also pleasing to the senses; they look good, feel good, even smell good. They are nice to have around, adding texture, shape, color, and a creative aura to the kitchen or dining room. So, don't hide them away in drawers and cupboards—hang them up, gather them in baskets or pots, place them on racks or open shelving. You'll be surprised how visitors to your kitchen will be drawn to pick them up, to heft and handle them. And what nicer compliment to the craftsman could there be than to have his work communicate so invitingly?

4.
Stirrers, Spoons, and Scoops

WOODEN SPOON

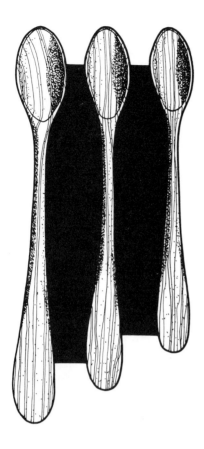

Whether the beverage you are making is hot or cold —a cool sangria drink, fresh iced tea with a few squirts of lemon, or a deep bowl of mulled wine for those late wintry afternoons—there is nothing more handy than a long-handled spoon for stirring. These spoons are noticeably thinner than most, and will fit easily inside many of your pitchers and glasses brimming with ice cubes. An added feature is the wide flare on the tip of the handle, which will give you a better grip and allows the spoon to rest on the flat of your hand for firm stirring jobs that require more control. Three spoon sizes are illustrated; try the large one first, then work down in size.

WOOD
Your best wood choice would be ash, maple, or well-seasoned Douglas fir. The wood, in any case, needs to be dry and should have a relatively close grain. This will minimize some of the staining, but do expect some discoloration, which will only give it a more unique character.

Once you have decided what wood you will use, buy piece(s) dimensioned to fit your needs as specified in the Illustration A. The large spoon shown in the pattern was actually cut from kiln-dried ash, 1¼ **by ½ by 9¾ inches**

(width, height, and length respectively). Note that the tolerances are very slight. This was done in order to cut down on your sanding time and effort. Therefore, when you are actually sawing the stock, proceed slowly for a more accurate and resourceful result. Smaller spoons are made from shorter stock, but are not a great deal thinner across the tip of the spoon, since this would only weaken its stirring/mixing effect.

EQUIPMENT
Coping saw
C-clamp or table vise
Spoon-bit gouge
Rubber or wood mallet
Surform flat file or medium double-cut file
Sandpaper: grades 120, 220, 280, 400 (aluminum oxide paper)
Steel wool: extra fine grade 000
Vegetable oil (or mineral or olive oil),
Soft, lint-free cloth
Pencil #2
Ruler

PROCEDURE
Illustrations A and B give general and specific dimensions for the large spoon. These dimensions will enable you to draw the proportions correctly with no guesswork. Once you have made complete drawings for both the top and side of the spoon on your tracing paper, transfer the drawing to the wood following the guidelines in Chapter 3. Clamp the wood upright in a table vise, or clamp flat, with several inches of the wood extending beyond the table's edge, by means of the C-clamp.

Begin sawing along the pencil line with the coping saw, making sure you stay a bit to the right (or outer) edge of the line. Proceed slowly to ensure a natural and smooth-flowing contour. In order to come full circle, adjust the C-clamp periodically to bring the uncut portion of the wood into position. Separate spoon from remnant. Once again, clamp the spoon to the work surface, and, lightly tap the spoon-bit gouge with the mallet to carve out the hollow area of the spoon. This hollow area measures 2½ inches in inner diameter lengthwise. The short taps must not be forceful, or you will most likely carve out the long sliver of wood that is to form the lip of the spoon. Bring your gouge upwards as you carve. This will give the concave part of the spoon a more natural contour.

The neck of the spoon, just behind the hollowed-out area, is naturally thinner than the end of the handle. Since this is the part of the spoon that receives the most stress during vigorous stirring, do not make it thinner than the recommended ¼-inch diameter.

Note that the handle has a graceful taper to it. This is achieved by cross-filing with the Surform flat file or smooth wood file in a diagonal direction, the entire length of the handle. The side view of the scaled drawing gives the correct proportions, which should also be clearly drawn on the stock. The tip of the handle tapers, ever so slightly, to give it a finished look and an overall more pleasing shape.

Begin sanding to remove all rough spots and unwanted high spots. Always sand in the direction of the wood's grain. If you must sand across the grain, do so with a light touch, making as few strokes as necessary to do the trick. Begin sanding with grade 120 flint or garnet sandpaper to remove all evidence of saw marks. Retain the overall shape you intended the spoon to have. You will quickly find out how abrasive this particular grade of paper can be, so sand slowly. Change to grades 220 and 280, respectively, to get at the more hard-to-reach areas, such as the hollow area and the underside, or "belly," of the spoon. Use the 400 grade to bring up the natural luster of the wood and to remove all traces of sanding marks created by the scoring of the grit of the previous grades. Rub the spoon with steel wool for a few minutes. Then, add three or four drops of vegetable oil to a clean, lint-free cloth. With a buffing motion, work the oil into the wood to lubricate the pores and add a natural patina to the wood's inherent color.

To make the other spoons pictured simply reduce the measurements to conform to your desired size. Repeat the steps just given, and, with a few hours in the shop in the morning, you will be stirring up all sorts of good things by noon.

One more thing: Don't hide these beauties in a drawer. When not in use, plant them in a jar filled with other similar items. They are good-looking and functional, and they should be shown off. Soon, you will be taking orders from admiring passersby who venture through your galley.

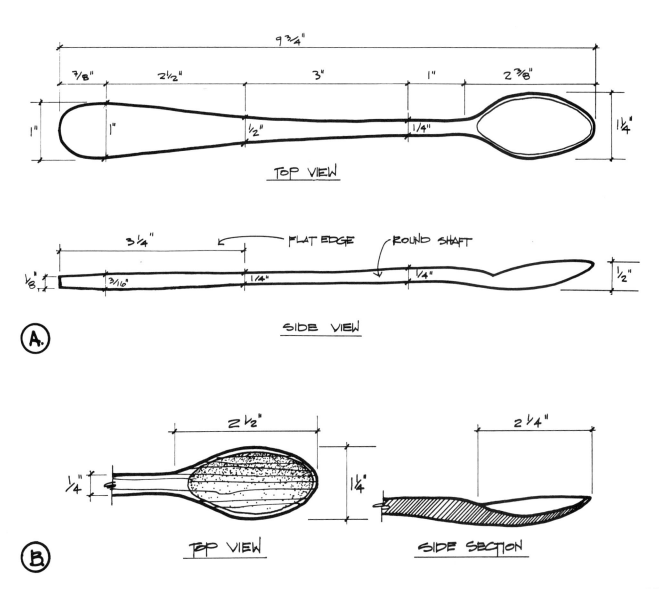

SPATULA SPOON

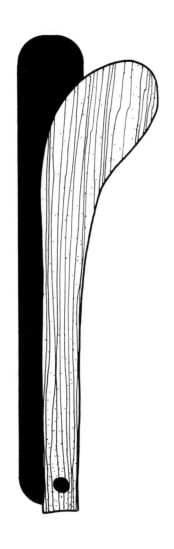

As the name implies, this utensil is a combination spoon —to be used for stirring, mixing, and blending—and spatula—for flipping or removing small biscuits, cupcakes, and other Lilliputian goodies from the oven. As far as blending is concerned, I have found that large stewing spoons do not really blend ingredients all that well. They tend to trap some of the finer and more delicate morsels in the concave portion. This minor annoyance can be obviated with the spatula spoon. Also the spatula spoon is a great deal easier to wash up after dried food has stuck to it. A quick rinse under the tap and a light scouring will remove the most tenacious particles.

WOOD
Beech, boxwood, olive, cherry, or any hardwood adaptable to the rigors of cooking make ideal choices for this project.

Look for a wood in your nearby lumberyard that is attractive in color and grain figuration; or, you might find a derelict tree that has been felled for kindling. Because of the wear and tear this utensil is likely to receive, do restrict your choice of wood to a hardwood. Occasionally, softwoods are fine to use in the making of your utensils. However, they are not going to give you the durable workhorse treatment you can expect from the harder woods. Your piece of wood should measure ¼ **by 2¼ by 8 inches.**

EQUIPMENT
Coping saw
C-clamp or table vise
Surform flat file or fine double-cut file
¼-inch drill bit and hand or power drill
Sandpaper: grades 120, 220, 280, 400 (aluminum oxide paper
Steel wool: extra fine grade 000
Vegetable oil (or mineral or olive oil)
Soft, lint-free cloth
Pencil #2
Ruler

PROCEDURE
The overall dimension of the wood before shaping is ¼ by 2¼ by 8 inches. Because of the natural curvature of the spatula spoon, there will be some waste once the utensil has been cut and separated from the surrounding stock. Following the illustration, draw the profile of the spatula spoon on tracing paper, making sure that the proportions and outline of the utensil conform to the suggested figures in the illustration. Transfer the drawing to the top side of the wood plank by following the directions in Chapter 3. After this has been completed, make a small dot with your pencil on the upper end of the wood to earmark the point where the ¼-inch hole will be drilled. The hole is, of course, optional, but may be useful if you want to hang the utensil when not in use.

Because sawing in a straight line is easier than sawing a curve, lock the wood stock upright in a vise, or clamp with a C-clamp in such a way that it extends outward from the workbench. Saw the back side (the long edge) of the spoon first. Do not attempt to curve the blade to make the forward curve of the spoon on this first cut. Rather, continue in a straight line, making sure the saw blade exits on the opposite end. It will be easier for you at this point to come in with the saw on an angle to cut the forward curve of the spoon. The third cut should be the inside one, which has a very gentle curve to it. Note that this curve is not identical to the outside one, but slopes with less of a radius. It is this subtle difference that makes the spatula spoon so functional. Like the keel of a boat or a hockey stick, this slight incongruity is essential to the success of its design, and its design is predicated on its function. The last cut is reserved for the round shape of the spoon's tip. Any slight bulge or deviation from the penciled line can be easily removed with the file and cleaned up with 120 sandpaper. Work the wood with steel wool to a smooth finish.

Drill through the wood with the ¼-inch drill bit at the marked spot. Hardwood is not likely to splinter as the drill bit exits on the other side, because the drilling process is done slowly. If in doubt, back the handle with a scrap of wood or piece of heavy tape, and drill through to the scrap or through the tape. This technique will minimize slight splintering and is a helpful hint to keep in mind. Finish the spoon by rubbing in oil with a soft cloth, and, if you will be hanging the spoon, place a thin piece of leather through the hole and knot it. (String or braiding tend to absorb foods and stain.)

And there it is . . . the spatula spoon, a most useful tool. Lest you underestimate the importance of this or any other wooden utensil consider this account of a medieval kitchen:

"In the larger establishments of the Middle Ages, cooks . . . gave their orders from a high chair. . . . Each held a long wooden spoon, with which he tasted . . . the various comestibles . . . and which he frequently used as a rod of punishment on the backs of those whose idleness and gluttony too largely predominated over their diligence and temperance."

—*Old American Kitchenware*

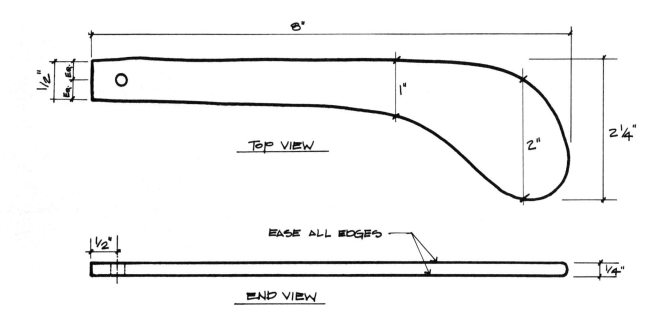

TOP VIEW

EASE ALL EDGES

END VIEW

BAMBOO BALLOON WHISK

The whisk performs an interesting feat. It transforms one single stroke into a series of motions, bringing an abundance of air pockets to egg whites, light batters, omelettes, and the like. I prefer this bamboo whisk over the metallic kind for a simple reason. I find the sound of the metal wires against a metal bowl particularly nerve-racking and much prefer the quietness of the wooden counterpart. Its lightness and agility are equally desirable; and I don't feel like I have sparred ten rounds with a thick batter after I've used it.

WOOD

The bamboo whisk is made of three pieces—two are bamboo rods, and the remaining piece constitutes the handle, into which are inserted the four ends of the two bamboo rods.

Wood for the handle should be a smooth hardwood. If you choose to carve the handle, as I did, you might use a favorite piece of oak, hickory, ash, maple, or beech. Indeed, they are hard woods, but, equipped with a sharp knife and a penchant for whittling, you can have your handle in an hour's time, sans hole, which will have to be drilled. In any event, **the wood of your choice should measure 4 inches plus in length, and 1 inch in height and width. The bamboo rods must measure at least 11½ inches in length, ⅛ inch wide.** Florists, hobby shops, craft-supply stores, and raffia and cane suppliers are excellent sources for these round bamboo rods. They cost next to nothing and have the marvelous ability to be bent and literally tied in a knot after they have soaked for a couple of hours—all without the least bit of splintering or cracking.

EQUIPMENT

Coping saw
½-inch drill bit and hand or power drill
C-clamp or bench vise
Wood-carving knife (pocket knife) with a sharp blade
Waterproof white glue (or resorcinol wood glue)
Sandpaper: grades 120, 220, 280, 400 (aluminum oxide paper)
Steel wool: extra fine grade 000
Vegetable oil (or mineral or olive oil)
Soft, lint-free cloth
Pencil #2
Ruler

PROCEDURE

If all facets of your wood are true, then proceed to the drilling step. If the wood is irregular, file the wood to make all sides parallel with one another.

Secure the wood block in a vise or by means of a C-clamp. Locate the center of the block and mark it with a pencil. Using the ½-inch drill bit, bore a hole in the upright end of the block to a depth of 1½ inches. Remove the wood from the vise and ease all edges for a smooth grip. If you are to carve the handle, note the dimensions given in the Illustration A and follow these for best results. Periodically, grasp the handle to check for fit and comfort. When the handle is satisfactory, start sanding with the coarsest of the sandpapers, in this case, grade 120. Work up through the finer grades, finishing with the steel wool. Do not apply the oil until you have installed the tendrils and all steps have been completed.

Soak the bamboo rods for 2 hours in warm water. They must be fully immersed for optimum absorption. Remove from the soaking tub and test the rods for flexibility by forming loops. If they bend without resisting, they are ready. With one hand, hold the handle upright, and, with the free hand, insert both ends of one rod to the maximum depth of the handle's hole. Repeat this step with the remaining rod. The fit must be snug. Point the nozzle of the glue dispenser into the hole and squeeze gently. A small amount is all that is required; the subsequent expansion as the bamboo dries will secure the ends in a very tight fit. Let the whisk stand overnight.

As the bamboo dries, you will note the ciliated fibers. These are characteristic of this type of bamboo. Do not sand them. They are delicate hairs and will actually aid the whipping activity.

After the whisk has dried, apply oil to the handle and rub with a dry, soft cloth to finish.

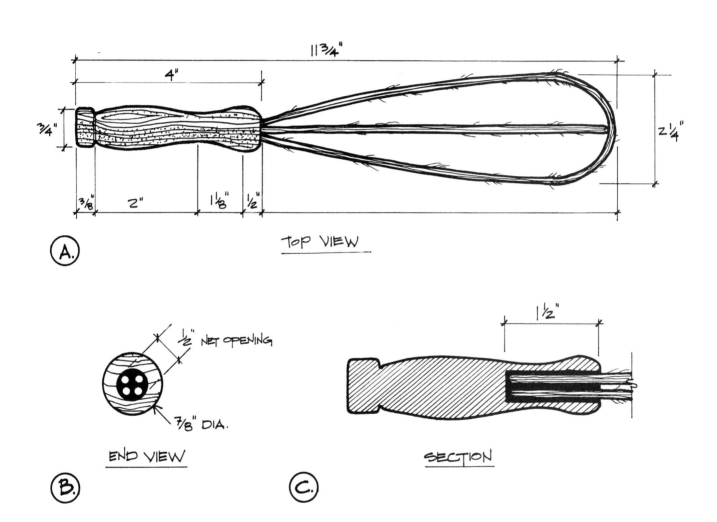

TOP VIEW

A.

END VIEW

B.

SECTION

C.

EGG SPOON

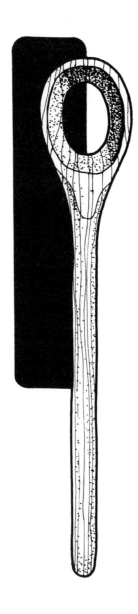

Lifting a hard- or soft-boiled egg from scalding water requires a spoon with a long handle. With such a spoon you can easily transport the egg, intact, to the dining table, with no boiling water on you, the floor, or the table. It is a useful addition to any cook's collection of kitchen utensils. Deceptively simple, very functional, and equipped with a hole that never needs to be mended, this centuries-old Scandinavian spoon also doubles as a stirring spoon for batter and thick stews. It is a perfect complement to the other long-handled utensils in the kitchen crock or mason jar. Stirring thick ingredients will no longer be a physical grind once you have discovered the pleasure and effect this egg spoon has on your culinary efforts. Directions for an Egg Cup project are on page 56.

WOOD

Birch is an attractive, light-colored wood that serves as a real workhorse in many wooden utensil designs. Its short, but tight, grain and its ability to withstand lots of abuse makes it an ideal choice when it comes time to consider what wood you should use. An equally satisfactory option or two would be cherry or even black walnut, which is readily available on the east coast of the United States. Mahogany, maple, or ash are also good choices. **Choose a plank ½ by 2 by 12 inches** of any of the recommended woods.

EQUIPMENT

Coping saw
C-clamp or table vise
Spoon-bit gouge
Rubber or wood mallet
Wood-carving knife (pocket knife) with a sharp, no less than 2-inch blade
Surform flat file or medium double-cut file
Sandpaper: grades 120, 220, 280, 400 (aluminum oxide paper)
Steel wool: extra fine grade 000
Vegetable oil (or mineral or olive oil)
Soft, lint-free cloth
Pencil #2
Ruler

PROCEDURE

Examine the top and side view of Illustration A. Note the overall configuration of the spoon, its general appearance, and the placement of the hole. Make a tracing of the tool on tracing paper. If your utensil is to be larger than the one illustrated, note that the dimensions given are not the actual size of the drawing, so adjust accordingly. Transfer (see Chapter 3), the top and side drawings to the respective top and side areas of the wood and prepare to saw. With the wood clamped by means of a table vise (or C-clamp) saw the shape as defined by the penciled line. The coping saw must be worked carefully, as there is little tolerance for error. A few jiggles here and there will not drastically affect your design, but accuracy should be stressed.

Once the wood has been parted from the remnant, you will have what, in effect, resembles a flat paddle. Sketch in the scooped area with a pencil, and, with the spoon-bit gouge and mallet, lightly tap the gouge to create a concave shape, making sure that only very small chips are removed at a time. The angle of the wall of the spoon is about 45 degrees. If, after one too many taps with the mallet, you have gone through the spoon in the concave part . . . good! You now have that quality that makes this spoon unlike so many others, and you have done so with true purpose.

With your knife (the blade must be razor sharp), begin to carefully enlarge the hole by removing thin parings of wood in a circular fashion, until you have made an opening 1⅛ by 1¾ inches large, resembling an ellipse. No rough edge around the lip of the opening must remain. The pocket knife is easily maneuvered, and it is still the best tool for this whittling technique.

You must now attend to the handle. The tip is rounded by means of the file. Whether you use the Surform or the smooth wood file, carefully work it over the top, sides, and bottom of the spoon to maintain the ½-inch diameter called for. The handle, which was originally square and flat, is now transformed into a smooth rod for easier gripping and turning. Next, file flat the 1-inch portion which, in effect, connects the handle and the depressed area of the spoon. Continue to flatten all the way around the upper lip of the spoon. Turn the spoon over and flatten the underside by means of carefully filing to remove any traces of what was once the "belly."

Proceed to lay out the required sandpapers, steel wool, and vegetable oil. Beginning with the coarsest grade, lightly sand the entire spoon, including the inner rim of the hole. Continue this activity with the other sandpapers, until you have gone from the coarsest to the smoothest of your sandpapers. Take a moment to run your fingers over the entire utensil before you proceed to the steel wool. How does it feel? Does it conform to the shape of your hand, your fingers? Do rough areas remain? Is the overall balance just right for you? If all is satisfactory, then spend a few minutes polishing the wood's surface with the steel wool. In a few rare instances, inferior steel wool or steel wool that has been previously used on metals may impart a slight discoloration to light-colored wood, so use new steel wool to offset any problems.

If vegetable oil is not handy, you should use mineral oil or olive oil in its place. For best absorption, allow the utensil to stand in a can of one of the above oils overnight. Next day, vigorously rub the tools to remove any remaining trace of oil before using.

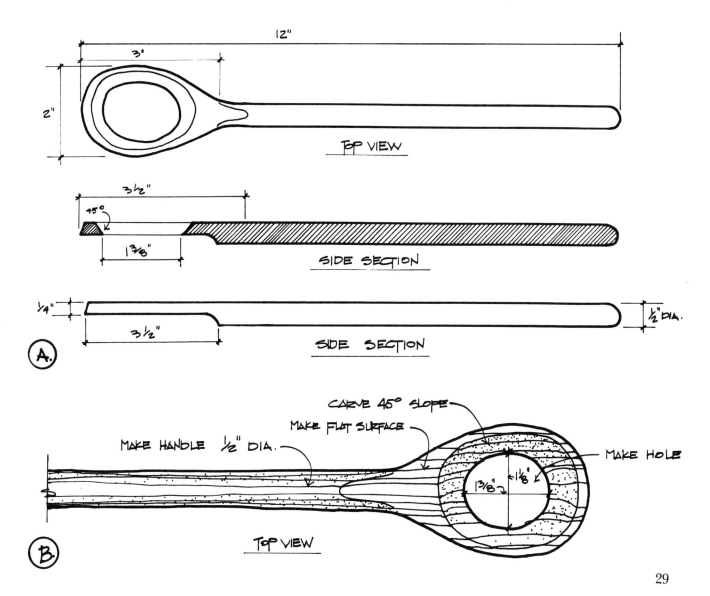

12"

3"

2"

TOP VIEW

3½"

45°

1⅜"

SIDE SECTION

¼"

3½"

½" DIA.

SIDE SECTION

(A.)

CARVE 45° SLOPE

MAKE FLAT SURFACE

MAKE HANDLE ½" DIA.

MAKE HOLE

1⅜" 1⅛"

(B.) TOP VIEW

STEWING SPOON AND DRAINING SPOON

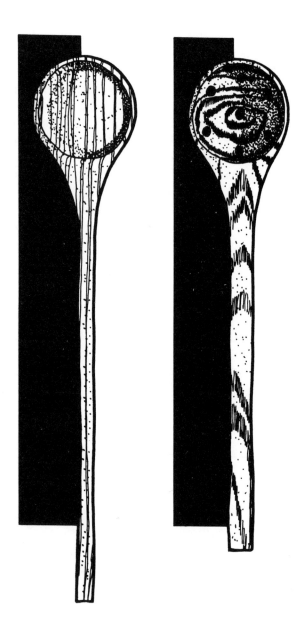

Many wooden implements have their origin in the Scandinavian countries, particularly Sweden, which produces so many of the fine contemporary designs we are seeing more and more of in this country. The spoons illustrated here, although not directly attributed to any one culture, depict some of the grace and streamlined simplicity of Scandinavian products. Both spoons are identical except that one has a perforated scoop and serves a different purpose. For simplicity, you might make both items the same size. In effect, you will make two spoons, one of which is carried a little further by drilling holes in the scooped portion to drain off excess water and juices. I will describe how to make the spoon, and then add remarks for drilling the holes.

WOOD

As with so many of the other spoons, stirrers, paddles, and forks, it is best to use a hardwood, such as olive, lemon, birch, maple, or oak. If you plan carefully, there is no need to resort to a lot of cutting and drilling beyond what is necessary to make the tool. Therefore, obtain wood that is close in dimension to the finished product before cutting and sanding are begun.

If you plan to make both utensils at the same time, simply double up the quantity of wood, but proceed as if you are making one spoon. You will need a piece of one of the above-mentioned woods, **cut to 1 by 3 by 13 inches.** Check to be sure that all sides are parallel and that the wood is not warped. The grain should follow the direction of the length of the spoon.

EQUIPMENT

Coping saw
C-clamp table vise
Spoon-bit gouge
Rubber or wood mallet
Surform flat file or smooth wood file
Sandpaper: grades 120, 220, 280, 400
   (aluminum oxide paper)
Steel wool: extra fine grade 000
¼-inch drill bit and hand or power drill
Vegetable oil (or mineral or olive oil)
Soft, lint-free cloth
Pencil #2
Ruler

PROCEDURE

See Chapter 3 for directions and draw the spoon on tracing paper. The length is 13 inches. Transfer the drawing to the top surface of the wood plank, following the directions. On the side of the wood, indicate with pencil approximately where and how deep the scooped-out portion is to be. You will refer to this by eye and touch as your carving slowly approaches the measuring line.

With a sharp coping saw and with the wood firmly clamped, proceed to cut out the spoon from the wood block. As with the other spoons given in the book, this one will at first resemble a long paddle. How you work the wood determines the overall and final shape. In the top view of the illustration note that the inner diameter of the spoon measures 2½ inches. The spoon has a wall of thickness measuring ¼ inch all the way around the rim. It is possible to draw a freehand circle around the inner circle to act as a guideline to follow as you carve with the spoon-bit gouge. First, clamp the wood to the worktable, then gently tap the gouge with a mallet to scoop out small chips of wood. Slowly, the concave area will take form. Halfway down check by sight to determine how much deeper you need to go before the carving and scooping stops. I recommend a ¾-inch depth for the scoop.

You will need to sand the hollowed-out area with coarse sandpaper (120) to smooth the inner surface. After that, sand the entire utensil on all surfaces to remove any possible rough spots or splinters.

For the draining spoon, note the location of the holes in the illustration and mark with a pencil to match. Proceed to drill a total of seven holes equidistant from one another. The spacing and placement is not critical. However, the holes should not be too close to one another, as this would only serve to slow the draining of the water. (Typical spacing of the holes (⅞ inch) is shown in the scaled drawing.) Sand any rough spots that result from drilling, especially the ones that may appear on the bottom of the spoon, where the drill bit came through.

Any of the oils may be vigorously rubbed into the utensil after all sandings with recommended grades of sandpaper and steel wool have been completed. With a clean, lint-free cloth, work the oils into the wood. This may take more than one operation, as hardwoods are not as thirsty as some of the more open-grained softwoods.

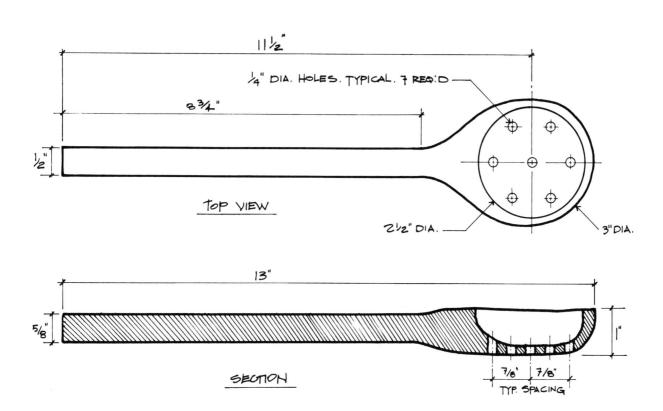

BAMBOO GRAIN AND FLOUR SCOOP

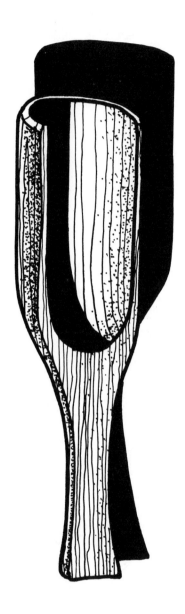

Originally conceived in Japan, the grain scoop is one of the most clever and simplest of cooking utensils to make, provided that you are fortunate enough to have some large pieces of bamboo at your disposal. The scoop becomes all the more useful when made in sets of ascending or descending sizes. This is relatively easy to do, since bamboo is jointed, making it wider at the base and narrower at the top. Graduated sizes of the joints make one long stem the perfect raw material for a set of four to six scoops of varied capacity. Bamboo utensils are unpretentious, light in the hand, and some species are extremely hard, making them practically impossible to dent or break. The example here is a typical one; you may want to modify the measurements to conform to any bamboo you find that is either smaller or larger.

WOOD

Any bamboo becomes hard after a few weeks of drying time in a warm environment. Some of the softer species tend to crumble under pressure, and it is this type that is not as useful as the harder variety. You will need **one jointed shoot over 5 inches in length. An ideal outer dimension width would be 1½ inches.**

EQUIPMENT

Coping saw
Wood-carving knife (pocket knife) with a sharp blade
Sandpaper: grades 120, 220, and 280
Ruler

PROCEDURE

Select one good section of the bamboo shoot, and cut out a 5-inch piece. Examine the inner hollow, a natural configuration of the grass, and note the bottom of what will become the concave portion of the scoop. Does it resemble the inner hollow of Illustration B? If so, then proceed to cut the shoot directly in half along the long axis. The shape of the handle is made by cutting in further with the coping saw, with the butt end ultimately measuring ¾-inch across. If you prefer a long-handled scoop, simply extend the measurement of the handle to meet your particular need. This is a nice variation for those hard-to-reach areas of large flour or sugar sacks tucked away in the back of the pantry.

Once all cuts have been made, there remains practically no further shaping to speak of. The inherent shape of the bamboo, its node and segmentation, makes it one of the most natural tools of its kind. It seems like an instant utensil, which it practically is.

Because the bamboo has been removed from the soil and has had a long curing or drying time outside of the average lumber mill, it is a good idea to wash the piece of bamboo in hot water to remove all traces of vegetation that might inadvertently still cling to the grass.

The edges of the scoop should be slightly sanded. Easing all edges makes a more comfortable grip possible and keeps the bamboo from splintering if it is going to get occasional rough treatment. It is not necessary to seal or oil the scoop in any way. The natural hardness of the exterior will serve as its own finish. Nothing beats hard bamboo for durability and longevity. You will have this handy scoop for a long time.

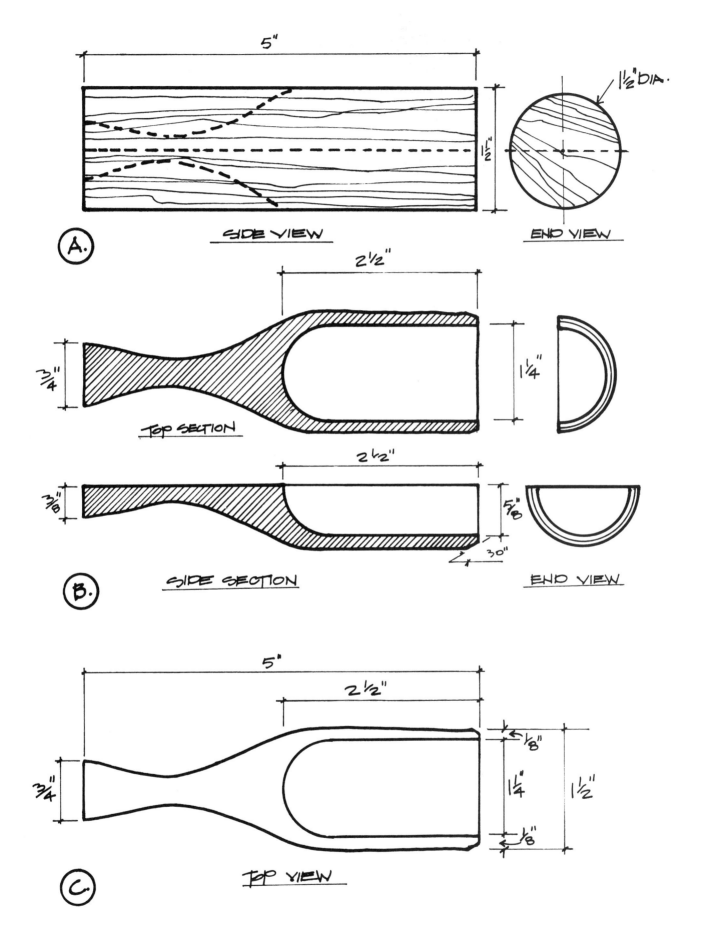

5"

1½"

1½" DIA.

A. SIDE VIEW   END VIEW

2½"

3/4"

1¼"

TOP SECTION

2½"

3/8"

5/8"

30"

B. SIDE SECTION   END VIEW

5"

2½"

3/4"

1/8"

1¼"

1½"

1/8"

C. TOP VIEW

33

BAMBOO WATER LADLE (HISHAKU)

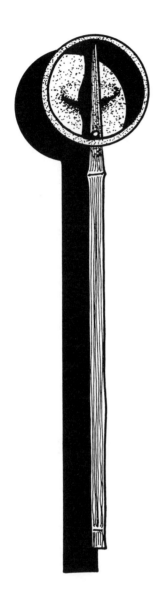

The Japanese Tea Ceremony is intrinsically a simple thing. The refinements that have arisen within its framework are numerous and baffling to the Western mind. Ultimately, the ritual is an attempt to move away from artifice. Its prescribed utensils are also simple and made of common materials, such as bamboo, iron, pottery, and the like. The ladle is used to draw hot water from the metal cauldron and poured into the small tea cup. I have observed several tea ceremonies and have never failed to be moved by the attention to detail and custom that host and guest bestow upon one another.

The ladle is used to draw hot water from the metal cauldron and pour it into the small tea cup. You will no doubt create your own uses for this special wooden utensil, as I have. I find it useful for ladling hot mulled wine and clear soups.

WOOD

Three pieces of bamboo make up the ladle—the handle, the cup, and the locking key, called the "retainer plug." The handle and cup may vary in size; the plug keeps the handle stable and connected to the cup. **I recommend using a larger section of bamboo, say 2 to 3 inches in diameter for the cup. The handle should measure 15 to 18 inches in length and ½ inch in diameter,** which is easily cut from a long shoot of leftover bamboo. The plug will need to be cut after the other steps have been completed.

EQUIPMENT

Coping saw
Wood-carving knife (pocket knife) with a sharp blade
⅛- and ⅜-inch drill bits and hand or power drill
Sandpaper: grades 120, 220, 280, 400
   (aluminum oxide paper)
Pencil #2
Ruler

PROCEDURE

Illustration A depicts one section of a large bamboo shoot. The cup will be cut out from this section and it is imperative that the two required cuts be made with a sharp coping saw in just the right places. Each joint of the bamboo shoot terminates in a closed membrane, which for us will be the cup's bottom. Note that the initial cut must include one intact membrane. To ensure best results in obtaining the membrane, cut ⅛ inch just below the thin joint (where the bamboo turns inward to form a "waist"). This way, you are most likely to include this crucial part. Measure 2 inches down from this first cut and make the second saw cut, thereby cutting free one complete section of the shoot. This is the cup of the ladle. Examine the inside to see that all surfaces of the cup are intact—no cracks, pinpoint holes, or overly thin bottom.

Drill a ⅜-inch hole through the cup ½ inch down from the top rim. With an imaginary line, determine where the opposite point will be directly across from this hole and make the shallowest of indentations at this new point on the inner wall. This dent will hold the tip of the handle in place. The indentation is best made with the tip of the knife. The tendency with a drill is to bore too deeply, risking a second, unwanted hole.

The handle measures 18 inches from tip to tip. Pick one end, measure back approximately 4 inches, and begin to shape the tip with a knife. A gentle taper that allows a snug fit in the cup's hole and permits the tip to nestle on the opposite wall of the cup is your objective. The cup's hole was made with a perfectly round drill. Your tapered handle must be made to fill that hole, with the same diameter and circumference in order to prevent leaks. Cut and taper with the knife, alternately sanding with 120 sandpaper.

When a proper fit has been achieved, mark the exact location on the tapered portion of the handle where the ⅛-inch hole for the plug is to be made. Drill through the handle and form a retainer plug to fit. The plug is best installed with a little manual force, since tapping with a

tool will most likely split the handle. The end of the tapered handle is seated in the indentation and needs no gluing. Sand all surfaces and ease all edges of the handle.

Lower and raise the ladle portion in a pot of boiling water to remove any impurities and to cause swelling of the wood. Repeat several times. And soon, the handle, by virtue of fit and expansion, will create a waterproof seal.

Several graduated sizes of the Japanese Water Ladle make a disarmingly beautiful wall display. They will bring a special atmosphere to your kitchen and invite many compliments and inquiries, too.

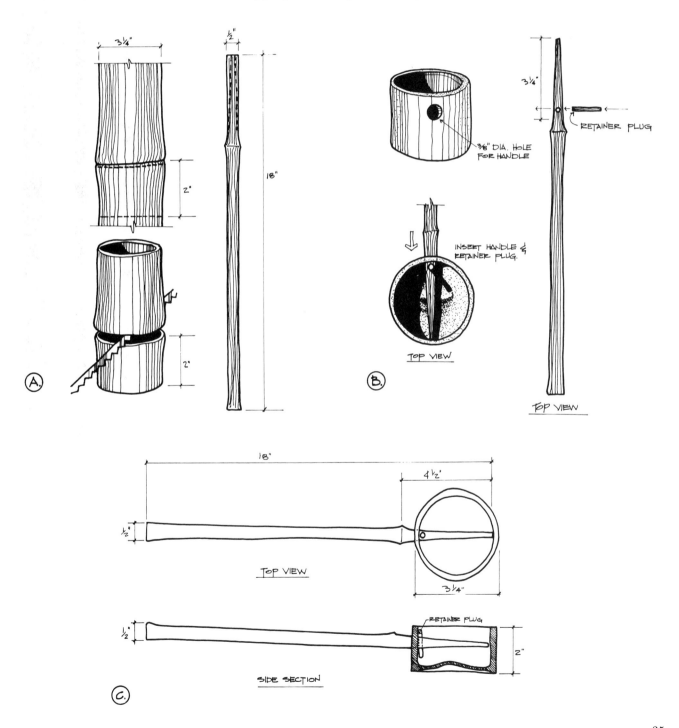

BAMBOO APPLE BUTTER SCOOP

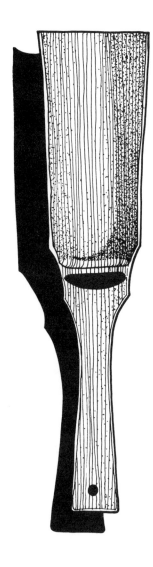

Feast your eyes on this implement. What at first appears to be an incongruous marriage of function to form is really an ideal match. Originally used by the Shakers for stirring their large vats of apple butter and other apple products (the scoop was employed to keep the butter from sticking to the bottom of the kettle and for spooning small quantities into equally small crocks for distribution), the scoop is equally handy for retrieving large quantities of rice, dried kibble, flour, grain, or sugar from oversized burlap sacks or storage tubs. Actually, the bamboo apple butter scoop makes other large scoops pale by comparison. Its size, a full 11 inches long, indicates the volume of dried or puried food it will hold.

The scoop, made from one piece of bamboo, can be made more concave by cutting the bamboo in half, lengthwise. Illustration A shows the end view and the actual portion for the scoop intended here.

WOOD

I have used bamboo because of its shape and hardness. The diameter of the bamboo shoot determines the width of the scoop. Try to find the widest ones possible to make the larger scoops, which are more useful for scooping large amounts of dried goods. **The width of the handle usually measures ¾ to 1 inch**, since it is formed from only a small part of the overall bamboo tube, as depicted in the top view of Illustration A.

The bamboo you select must be dry and sound. If the base of the plant has been soaked in water continuously for several weeks, it is likely to be weak and to further deteriorate.

EQUIPMENT

Coping saw (or any small-toothed saw)
Wood file with small teeth for fine sanding
Sandpaper: grades 120, 220, 280
¼-inch drill bit and hand or power drill
C-clamp or table vise
Wood-carving knife (pocket knife) with sharp blade
Rulers

PROCEDURE

Bamboo is composed of interconnecting joints, which can be obscured by a thin, papery sheath, easily removed to expose the juncture of the joints.

Select an 11-inch strip of bamboo stem that includes the ringlike joints, which becomes the back end of the scoop portion of the utensil. The remaining bamboo will make up the handle. In Illustration B, both views show an approximate relationship of handle to scoop. The scoop measures 5 inches, the taper of the node measures about 1 inch, and the handle measures 5 inches. Use a longer bamboo stem for an extended handle.

Clamp the hollow stem upright by means of a table vise. If you use C-clamps, then insert the stem in between two blocks, each 1 by 3 by 3 inches, and stand the stem upright. The wood and the tightened clamps provide the required rigidity to cut the bamboo lengthwise. Following the measurements prescribed in Illustration A, make a 5-inch coping saw cut along the long axis of the stem until the 1-inch measurement is reached. Then, slowly angle the saw blade downwards to reach the node (Illustration B, side view). Level the coping saw to keep the blade and bamboo surface parallel for a full 1 inch. Then, once again, angle the blade along a slight slope to form the handle. The handle is

⅜-inch thick. Continue to make a flat cut until the entire piece has been sawn. What may appear to be quite complicated in theory is actually very simple in practice. The front of the scoop is thicker than the back. By cutting into the wall of the bamboo, you make a handle that is easier to grasp, and you eliminate some of the extra weight of the utensil, while preserving the strength and thickness of the scoop portion, which receives all the work.

The overall taper to the scoop is achieved by making two cuts with the coping saw on both sides of the utensil. Each cut follows the illustration. Dimensions for the taper are given, but are only suggestions; your measurements may differ.

The hole in the handle is drilled with a ¼-inch drill bit and is done ½ inch back from the handle's edge. It is also centered. The drill bit must break through the other side without tearing the fibers beyond the capability of sand-paper repair. After holding the tool and checking it for fit, ease all edges with the three grades of recommended sandpaper. No further sanding or sealing is required.

The forward edge of the scoop can be tapered to achieve a sharper rim. This comes in handy for those thicker dried foods. A chain of coffee and tea stores uses this type of scoop with great success, while adding to the decor of the store. The beans are left in large burlap sacks with scoops up-ended for customers to use themselves. This is reminiscent of days when stores sold dry goods by volume, which was predetermined by the customer, not the producer.

No doubt the possibility of making graduated scoops has occurred to you by now. Simply cut up sections of bamboo that conform to a set of both small and large scoops. A simple rack, as presented on page 104, makes an excellent means of storing and displaying your hand-crafted efforts.

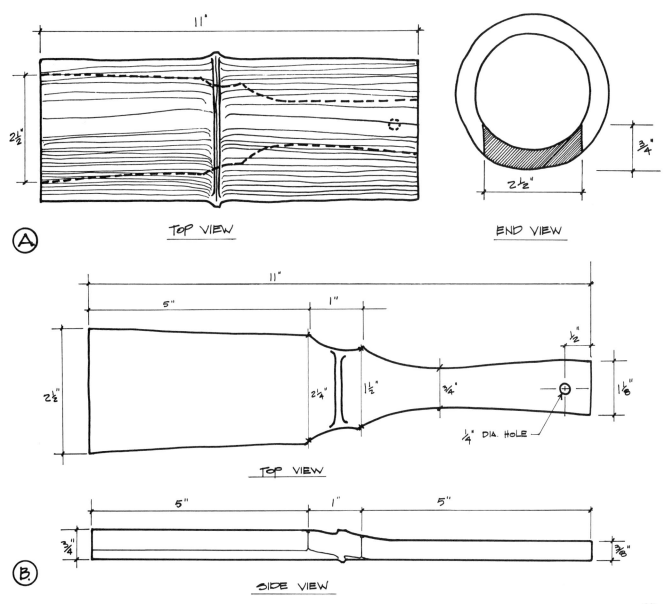

TOP VIEW

END VIEW

Ⓐ

TOP VIEW

¼" DIA. HOLE

SIDE VIEW

Ⓑ

BAMBOO TEA WHISK

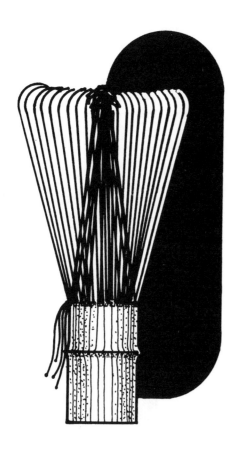

The Japanese *chasen,* or tea whisk, is an enchanting device. At a glance, it is hard to believe that this delicate, budlike creation comes from just a single piece of bamboo. The tea whisk brings with it a long tradition of use in the legendary Japanese Tea Ceremony, where its gentle whirling combines the finely powdered tea with hot water. Still produced by hand in Japan by only a few craftsmen, the tea whisk can have from thirty-two to one hundred and twenty splines, depending on its intended use. The version presented here is but a simplified one to indicate the procedure. You can use the technique to make a variety of whisks, fine to coarse, small to large—whatever suits your fancy. You will find the whisk a joy to use in stirring and combining any number of ingredients, and it makes a real conversation piece when on display.

WOOD AND OTHER MATERIALS
Bamboo is available in a variety of species. In Japan, various bamboos are used for whisks, including white, smoked, spotted, and green, to accommodate variations in tradition. Choose a piece that appeals to you in color and pattern. You will need **1 piece 4½ inches long by 1 inch in** diameter (see Illustration A for an indication of node position relative to length). You will also need approximately **1 yard of fine, strong string or heavy thread** in a neutral shade or a color to complement the bamboo.

EQUIPMENT
Coping saw
Wood-carving knife (pocket knife) with a very sharp blade
Protractor
Bench vise or C-clamps plus 2 blocks of wood
Small, flat jeweler's files
Vegetable oil (or mineral or olive oil)
Pencil #2
Ruler

PROCEDURE
Cut the 1-inch diameter bamboo to a 4½-inch length, so that the node is 1½ inches from one end, as shown in Illustration A. This shorter section will be the handle of the whisk. Next, using the knife, peel off some of the outer rind from the longer portion. Dipping the stock into hot water for a few seconds may facilitate the peeling process. Hold the handle portion and rest the other end of the bamboo on the work surface. Peel away from you, rotating the bamboo and removing very thin parings.

Next, tie a string securely around the longer portion of the shaft about ½ inch from the node (see Illustration C). This will serve as a temporary binding and a guideline for your longitudinal splits. Mark the cut end of the longer portion of the bamboo into sixteen equal sections. One way to do this is to draw a 1-inch circle on paper and divide it, using a protractor. Another way: cut a larger circle and fold it exactly in half, then in half again and in half again. Then cut a 1-inch circle from the center of the folded piece, position either pattern on the end of the bamboo, and mark the stock at each fold or line.

Secure the bamboo upright in a vise or hold it securely with two wood blocks on either side held in place by C-clamps. Proceed to make the vertical splits by starting each split with the knife and working slowly downward toward the string. You may separate the split slightly with your fingers to encourage the splitting action, but work slowly and carefully, so that the splits are straight and do not continue past the string.

When all sixteen cuts have been made, separate the splines, so that they flare to about 1½ inches in diameter (see Illustration C). Next, split each spline concentrically, dividing it into an inner and outer portion. The outer portion should be thinner, about $1/16$ inch or less. The inner splines should be broken free and removed. Smooth the interior of the whisk where the inner splines were broken out, with a file, until you are satisfied with the results.

Bend the remaining splines outward to create the necessary flare (see Illustration D). Then, continue splitting each spline lengthwise. For a simple whisk, split each spline once, for a total of thirty-two. For a more delicate product, each spline can be split into four, six, or eight sections. Proceed very carefully with each split. Too much pressure can break a spline, which will leave an unsightly gap. For a very delicate whisk, shave the interior surface of the splines. This is done by removing the piece from the vise and laying it on the work surface, so that the splines are supported during the shaving process.

When the splines are completed, hold the whisk over steam for a minute. You can now remove the string. Then, shape the tips of the splines by curling them over and in with the fingertips. Do several splines at a time and continue on around the piece (see Illustration F).

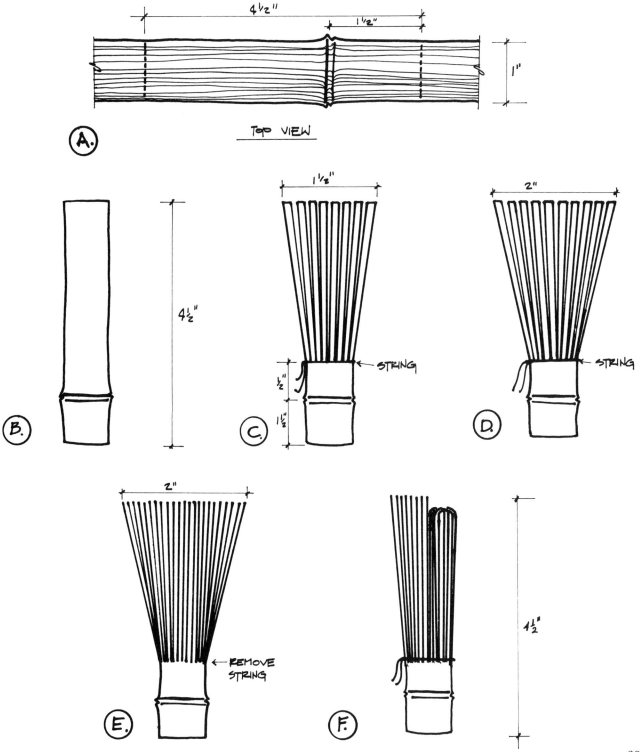

The last step in the creation of the tea whisk is to separate the splines into an inner core and an outer ring (see Illustration G). Cut a piece of string about 1 foot long. Place it in one of the splits, so that half the string is inside the whisk and half remains outside. Bring the two ends of the string around one spline and cross one end over the other at the next split (the interior string end passes to the outside, the outer string crosses to the inside). The next spline is skipped and encouraged inward by the string's crossing around the outside. Bring the string around the inside and outside of the next spline and cross again, forcing the fourth spline inward. Continue on around the whisk, every other spline being surrounded by the string, alternate splines being forced to the inside. When you reach the starting point, tie the string ends in a square knot (see any macrame book for square knot directions) and clip about ½ inch from the knot with scissors or a knife. Traditional whisks have a series of three such rows of stringing. However, this is not absolutely necessary. Repeating the procedure with another piece of string directly above the first one will add strength and stability to the whisk.

As the inner splines are drawn together, curve the curled ends around to form a sort of knotlike configuration. This gives the interior of the whisk a nice, finished look, and it keeps the inner core locked together when the whisk is in use.

As with many bamboo items, the whisk requires little or no real finishing. A little mineral oil applied to the handle and splines and rubbed in with the fingers will help keep the stock from drying out. Cleaning the whisk in warm, soapy water immediately after use will prevent any food residues from building up on the splines.

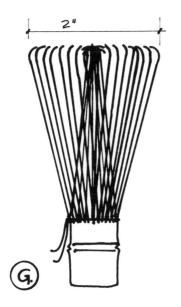

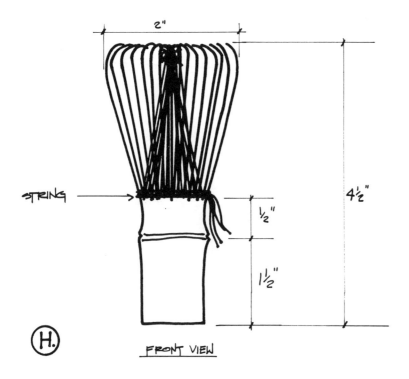

5.
Utensils for Serving

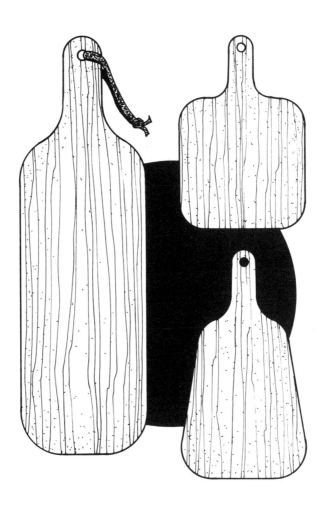

CHOPSTICKS

Traditional Japanese chopsticks are made of bamboo and are classified by shape and the location of the natural joint. The tapered end is used for pinching the food, while the top (sometimes with joint intact) provides balance. Lately, chopsticks made available to fans of oriental food have been made of inferior wood such as pine and, therefore, are not as highly regarded. By careful selection of quality wood and with a little bit of sanding you can make your own, which are certain to last longer and which will be far more attractive to the touch. While you have the materials laid out on the workbench, consider making a few pair for family and guests.

WOOD
Be sure that the wood you choose will withstand washing at high temperature with dish detergent.

Hardwoods such as oak, maple, and ash are perfect choices. Oak has a larger grain which tends to open up slightly when subjected to high-temperature dishwashers, but it gradually shrinks to its original form if allowed to dry by natural means. Maple is a workhorse and can hold up to lots of abuse. Ash, usually characterized by a longer grain with little evidence of pores, is just as reliable, but not as attractive if you are looking for wood with natural color contrast.

Your chopsticks may discolor after repeated washings. However, this only gives them a weathered look and in no way detracts from their appearance. If you would rather set the table with chopsticks that evince little sign of use, choose a darker hardwood such as walnut, ebony, or hickory. Avoid teak because of its undesirable oily properties.

Once you know which wood you want, decide on the number of chopsticks you are going to make. The ideal length for most people still remains the usual 8 inches. **For each pair of chopsticks you will need one piece of wood measuring 8 by ½ by 3/16 inches.** This dimension leaves little tolerance for extensive shaping or sanding. If you plan to really work the material, choose a stouter strip of wood to be worked to the above dimensions.

EQUIPMENT
Coping saw or small-toothed backsaw
Sandpaper: grades 80, 120, 220
Carborundum paper grades: 400 and 600
Pencil #2
Ruler

PROCEDURE
Dimension and mark the wood with the pencil and ruler. With the saw, very slowly cut the wood strip exactly down the middle. You may need to clamp the stock with the vise if the wood proves too shaky to be held upright on the work surface with one hand while the other saws. Illustration A shows the saw line and also illustrates the taper that will result from sanding the two front ends. All surfaces and edges are lightly sanded. Start with grade 80 sandpaper to remove potential splinters. Look closely for areas that are likely to split after a bit of use. Even the hardest of woods often have latent cracks or slight fissures which surface after use and submersion in water.

As you sand, give more emphasis to the front of the sticks paying particular attention to the fact that the sticks must retain some semblance of four sides. This ensures a tight grip on the food be it rice or bean sprouts. Illustration B shows the end view with all edges eased for easier and smoother handing.

Work your way through the higher and smoother grades of sandpaper and finish of with carborundum grade 600.

Do not apply any finish to the wood. For hygienic considerations the sticks should be washed in conventional dishwashers or should be slightly scrubbed in very hot water to remove small particles of food.

In any event, an occassional buffing with a soft cloth and safflower cooking oil will give a thirsty wood a near new look and extends the life of the chopsticks.

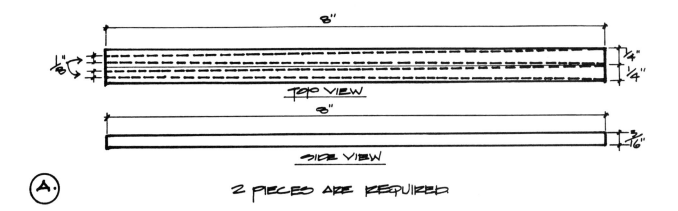

8"

¼"

⅛"

¼"

TOP VIEW

8"

SIDE VIEW

3/16"

A.

2 PIECES ARE REQUIRED

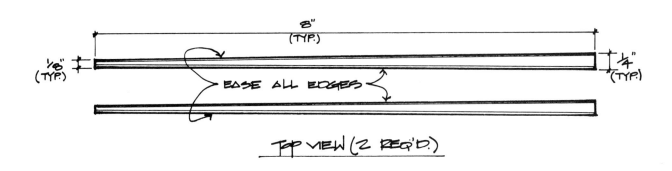

8"
(TYP.)

⅛"
(TYP.)

¼"
(TYP.)

EASE ALL EDGES

TOP VIEW (2 REQ'D.)

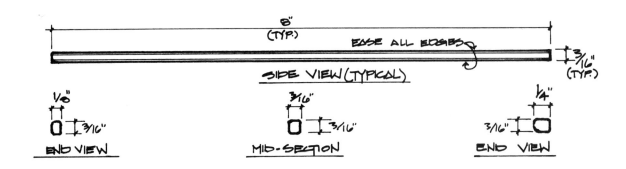

8"
(TYP.)

EASE ALL EDGES

3/16"
(TYP.)

SIDE VIEW (TYPICAL)

⅛"

3/16"

3/16"

3/16"

¼"

3/16"

END VIEW

MID-SECTION

END VIEW

B.

43

SAUERKRAUT FORK

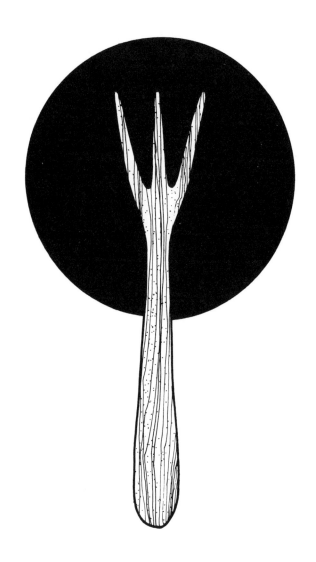

To keep sauerkraut from forever slipping off the fork, why not give it a lift by means of its own specially designed fork with widely spaced tines? Great for long spaghetti, noodles, and stringy vegetables, as well, this is one utensil you will want to keep stove-side for easy access. It's a cinch to make, and, like the ladle, has as many uses as you can imagine.

WOOD

Try beech, if available; also, eucalyptus or olive would be great, if you can locate a small piece or two. Other more available choices might be Douglas fir, oak, birch, or pine. Pine is the lightest and most inexpensive, but, since **you only need a good, flat piece measuring ¼ by 2½ by 12 inches**, you may want to splurge for the more exotic variety of wood. Examine the wood to eliminate any piece with checks (splits in the wood), knots, or warpage.

EQUIPMENT

Coping saw
C-clamp or table vise
Surform flat file or smooth wood file
Sandpaper: grades 120, 220, 280, 400 (aluminum oxide paper)
Steel wool: extra fine grade 000
Vegetable oil (or mineral or olive oil)
Small towel or short-napped cloth
Pencil #2
Ruler
Protractor

PROCEDURE

The sauerkraut fork is perhaps the easiest of all the utensils to make. It requires no woodworking flair of any kind, and yet, the result is such a useful one that you might want to try some variations to meet your unique needs for food preparation.

The first step is to draw the overall shape, both top and bottom surfaces, on tracing paper, following the directions in Chapter 3. Use a protractor to measure and mark specific angles. Make one drawing for each and transfer the tracing onto the wood's flat surface and the wood's edge respectively. With the wood firmly clamped by means of a table vise (or C-clamp, if it is to be gripped to the worktable), proceed to slowly saw the shape as defined by the penciled line. Needless to say, if you are using the C-clamp, give yourself a few inches of stock extending beyond the table's edge. I suggest starting with the handle. You will immediately find out if the wood is temperamental and difficult to cut (in which case you may want to proceed more slowly) or if it will be smooth sailing for the total cut. As you near the tine portion of the fork, reverse the stock and clamp the handle to the work surface. Approach the tip of each tine with the coping saw, and cut at 15-degree angles to the utensil's straight edge. This defines the separation of the tines and provides ample cutting room for the saw. The depth of each cut for the tines should measure 3 inches. This will give your fork the necessary length to lift the sauerkraut from anywhere in the pot onto an awaiting bowl or plate.

Approximately 1 inch separates each tine. Remember, this is not a salad fork, which has its own particular shape, but a utensil designed to do a special job. The relatively short, broad handle makes the fork easy to use.

Once the fork has been separated from the wood remnant, look closely to see if your fork's shape is an agreeable one. Any bulges you spot can be easily removed by means of coarse sandpaper.

Begin sanding with grade 120 garnet or flint sandpaper to eliminate rough spots and bulges. Sand with the grain of the wood. The utensil is a mere ¼ inch in thickness, so be judicious with your sanding efforts. There is a little to spare, but not much. Move on to the finer grades of sandpaper and then proceed to the steel wool. As you polish the wood with the steel wool, notice how smooth and lustrous the fork becomes. Pour a few drops of the vegetable oil into the steel wool pad and continue to polish, working the oil into the wood's surface. When you think it is as smooth as the wood will allow, rub the fork with a small towel or short-napped cloth. This will bring highlights to the wood and will remove any small pieces of steel wool that may inadvertently have lodged in the wood.

Boiling water is not injurious to the sauerkraut fork, so use the fork to scoop out heaps of delicious sauerkraut onto your plates. The nutritional value of cabbage, long preferred over the potato in Middle Europe, perhaps prompted the oft-quoted verse:

"The time has come," the Walrus said,
   "To talk of many things:
Of shoes—and ships—and sealing-wax—
   Of cabbages—and kings—"

Lewis Carroll

Use your sauerkraut fork in good health.

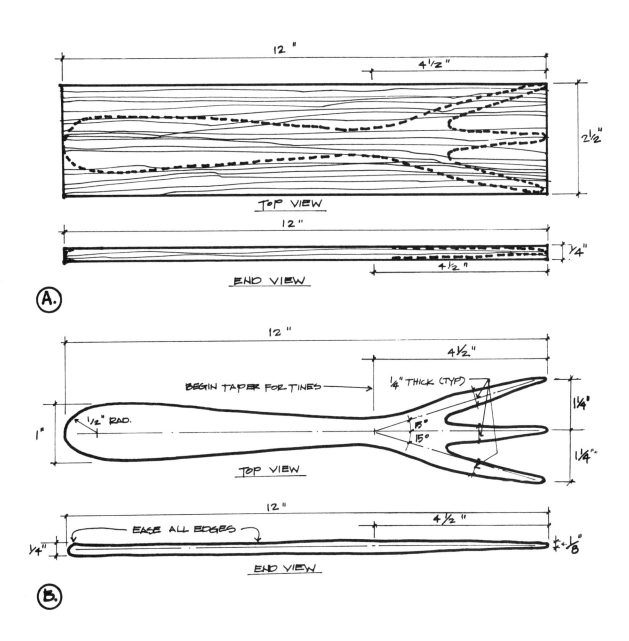

45

SPAGHETTI RAKE

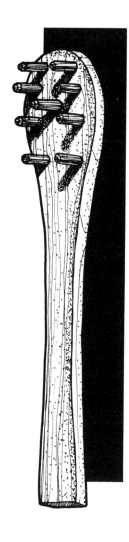

This curious anomaly of a utensil looks like everyone's favorite back scratcher, but it has a far nobler purpose here. It is used to lift steaming hot pasta from boiling water and to gently deposit it in its awaiting bowl or plates. The texture of the wood is just rough enough to lightly snag the strands, keeping them from rolling back into the pot (or worse, onto your guest's lap!) True pasta aficionados insist that pasta be served *al dente* (firm to the bite). This implement is one sure way to give you a morsel-size preview before a longer period of boiling is contemplated. The spaghetti rake also aids in keeping pasta strands separated as the water boils and cooks. (A teaspoon of olive oil added to the boiling water also helps prevent strands from clumping.)

Place the spaghetti rake high on your list of cooking utensils to make; you'll find one hundred and one uses for it. For food with finer strands, increase the number of plugs.

WOOD

Ten pieces of wood make up the spaghetti rake, **nine of which are 3/16-inch dowel plugs, which measure 1⅛ inches in length. The paddle portion (the tenth piece) is made from oak, ½ by 1¾ by 12 inches.** The design and function of the utensil does not weigh heavily on the choice of wood for the dowels. However, the choice should be made based on aesthetics (oak and cherry, for example), and availability of stock.

I recommend oak for the handle because it has the natural ability to withstand both hot and cold temperatures. (Some woods that are abruptly subjected to extreme changes of temperature are badly affected.) If left untreated with wood sealers, varnishes, shellac, and other synthetic finishes that should not be used in conjunction with eating utensils anyway, oak, after soaking in water, dries with a slightly rough surface. This rough surface, a minor characteristic, makes for a better grip, both in the hand and on the pasta.

EQUIPMENT

Coping saw
C-clamp or bench vise
3/16-inch drill bit and, hand or power drill
Sandpaper: grades 120, 220, 280, 400 (aluminum oxide paper)
Steel wool: extra fine grade 000
1 sheet of ⅛-inch graph paper
Pencil #2
Ruler

PROCEDURE

Begin by tracing the pattern of the spaghetti rake on tracing paper, paying particular attention to the overall design given. The illustration shows the exact placement of the pegs. Keeping in mind that the actual drawing is smaller than the actual rake, proceed to make an enlarged drawing on the graph paper. The instructions for how this procedure is done are found in Chapter 3. Once you have established where the holes are positioned on the graph paper, proceed to transfer the complete drawing on the top surface of the block of wood cut to the given specifications (see Chapter 3 again). The illustration gives you exact measurements, which can be easily laid out by simply copying the plan.

With the coping saw, cut out the flat piece of wood that serves as the "paddle" for the spaghetti rake. With the drill and drill bit, make nine holes, where indicated, to a depth of ⅛ inch each. This must be done with gentle pressure. Otherwise, you are likely to drill through the wood. A helpful suggestion: place a piece of masking tape around the drill bit above the imaginary ⅛-inch line. Then, drive the bit downwards until the wood surface and tape edge meet.

Beginning with the coarsest sandpaper, sand both sides and edges of the spaghetti blade. Finish sanding with the steel wool. Do not apply any oil to the wood, either at this point or when the utensil is finished, as you want to keep the wood grain open.

From a long dowel rod of ³/₁₆-inch diameter (an 11-inch dowel rod will do nicely), cut nine equal pieces, each measuring 1⅛ inches in length. On one end of each dowel plug, bevel the edge to a 45-degree angle around the full circumference. Use 280 grade sandpaper and sand the plugs individually until they are reasonably smooth. Do not use the finer sandpapers for this.

Insert each plug into its respective hole. If they won't go, use a wood mallet and lightly tap each one into place. If for some reason (such as over-sanding), the plugs are loose, you have a couple of choices. The first; apply a small amount of waterproof, nontoxic (white) glue to each hole, fit the plug, and allow to stand overnight. Hopefully, the wood will expand when the rake is subjected to boiling water and will permanently seal itself. The second: if the first method does not work or seems like it is too much of a bother, simply cut nine new plugs and sand the surface less.

For a utensil with a greater number of finer teeth for such things as string beans, very fine spaghetti, and even rice, consider modifying the number of plugs to meet your needs.

Keep the spaghetti rake in a ceramic crock next to the stove. It is good looking and will complement any array of utensils you care to display.

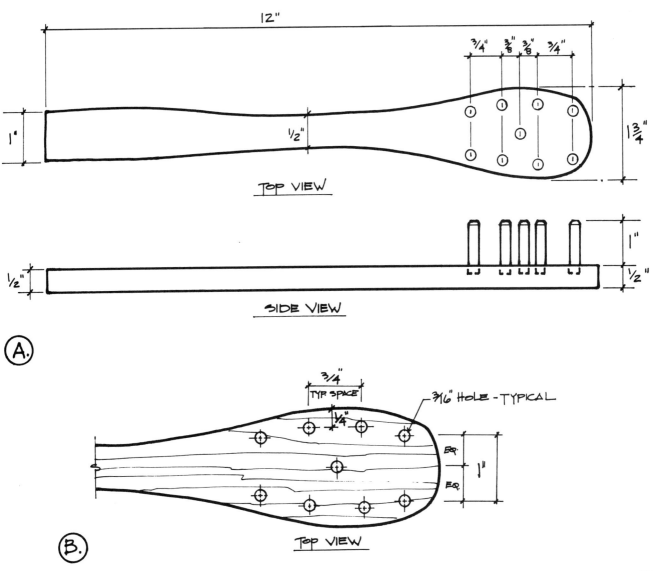

HONEY DIPPER

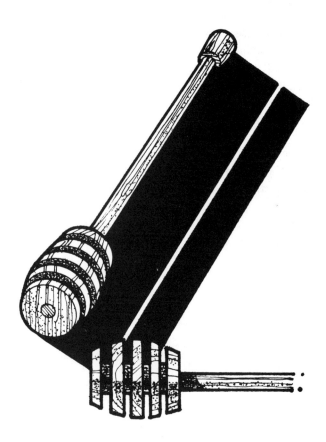

Watching the warm amber stream play off the end of the honey dipper is almost as satisfying as the taste of the honey itself. A delightfully handy item for transporting honey from pot or jar to the intended place without drips and drizzles, the dipper is so designed that, given a gentle twirling motion, it will hold the honey in its concavities. Then, when held still, the honey gently flows in and out over the rings. The design is based on the Italian *molinolo*, a tool used for swirling melted chocolate. Here, however, the rings are fixed and can be all the same diameter or shaped to an oval contour.

WOOD

You will need three dowels of three different sizes in ash or pine: **one 6 inches long by ¼ inch in diameter, one 1¼ inch long by ½ inch in diameter, and one at least ⅝ inch long by 1 inch in diameter for the washers.** You will also need a **wooden bead ⅝ inch in diameter.**

EQUIPMENT

Coping saw
C-clamp or table vise
¼-inch and ½-inch drill bits and hand or power drill
Sandpaper: grades 120, 220, 280, 400 (aluminum oxide paper)
Surform or flat wood file
Waterproof white glue
Cotton swab
Soft, lint-free cloth
Pencil #2
Ruler

PROCEDURE

Use a coping saw to cut the ¼-inch and ½-inch dowels to size, as indicated in Illustration A. Cut five washers from the 1-inch dowel, each ⅛ inch thick. To mark the dowel for cutting, place a piece of masking tape around the rod to serve as a guide, ⅛ inch back from the end of the dowel. Cut the first washer; replace the tape ⅛ inch back on the rod and cut the next washer. Proceed until all five washers have been cut.

Secure the ½-inch dowel in a vise, or, placing a block of wood on either side, hole it in place with a C-clamp, and drill a ¼-inch diameter hole lengthwise through the ½-inch dowel. Using the same ¼-inch drill bit, drill a hole in the wood bead to a depth of ¼ inch where it will be attached to the shaft. Next, drill a hole in the center of each wood washer, using the ½-inch bit.

When all the cutting and drilling is done, check to see that all the pieces fit together, as shown in Illustration B. Make any adjustments to ensure ease of assembly. Then, sand all parts, working from coarse to fine sandpaper. The washers will require the most work. You may wish to shape the washers so that the end of the dipper will have rounded contour, as shown in the illustration. If so, stack them together, clamp them firmly with a short piece of smaller diameter dowel or small wood block on each end (covering the hole), and proceed to shape the washers, tapering from the center toward each end, using a Surform or flat wood file. You may have to reposition the stock in order to work all sides uniformly. After shaping, complete the sanding and then clean all pieces with a tack rag or a soft, clean cloth.

To assemble the honey dipper, first glue the shaft and bead together, using white glue on the tip of the shaft and inserting it into the bead. Then, glue the ½-inch dowel onto the other end of the shaft the same way, being sure the ends of the two dowels are flush. Wipe off any excess glue with warm, soapy water and a clean cloth. Allow the glue to dry thoroughly.

Mark the ½-inch dowel for the placement of the washers as illustrated in Illustration B. Apply glue to the interior of the hole in the first washer and slip it into place. (If you have shaped the washers, be sure to get them in the right order.) Clean off any excess glue with a cotton swab and proceed to position the next washer. Be careful not to displace the washers already on the dowel, as you add each new one. Allow the finished piece to dry thoroughly.

Since the honey dipper will be used directly with food, no toxic finishing material should be applied. The dipper may even be left in the honey pot when not in use, though it should be washed occasionally, with warm, soapy water and a long-bristled brush to clean between the washers. The preservative nature of honey will keep the end of the dipper in good condition, and oil from the hand will help to lubricate the handle portion of the wood. If you wish, season the whole tool with a light application of mineral oil, applying just a touch to the washers and areas between them with a cotton swab. Wipe after oiling with a clean, soft cloth.

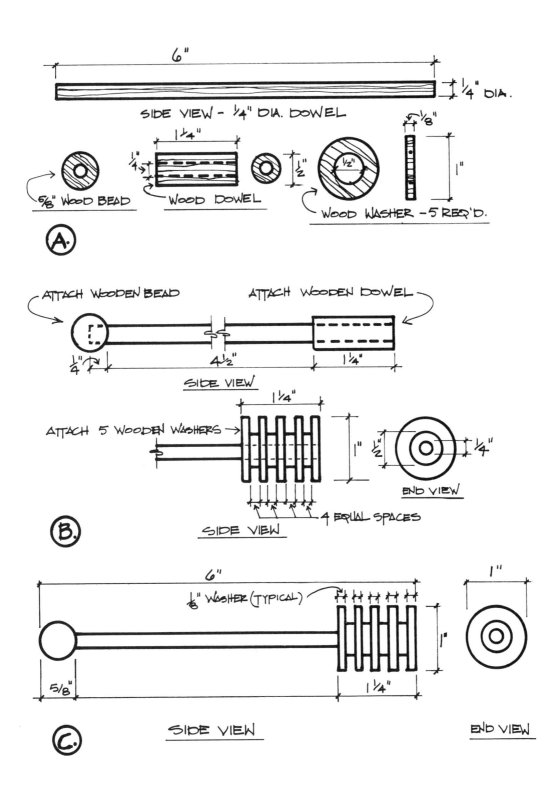

TACO TWEEZERS

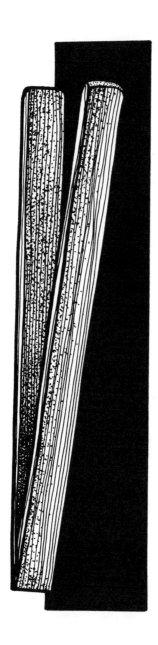

No, tacos do not have splinters, but they can at times be too hot to handle, particularly when they have been fried with cooking oil. At last, here is a simple device to solve the problem, as pleasant to look at as it is to use. The bamboo allows easy insertion beneath the tortilla without fear of scraping a Teflon surface or tearing the flour tortilla, which is more fragile than the corn variety.

These tweezers are excellent for removing fish bones from salmon, trout, mackerel, or any fish for that matter. Use the taco tweezers to remove a pouch of heat-and-serve vegetables from a pot of boiling water, or even to get at that stray English muffin lodged in the bottom of the toaster.

There are a thousand uses for such a gadget. Consider making them for gifts, or make several for your own dinner guests.

WOOD

The wood you choose should have a springy quality, which materials like bamboo, sugar pine, Douglas fir, and other softwoods all have. By shaving or cutting the wood thinly, much of the spring is created, but the trick is to preserve the strength a utensil like this should possess. **Both pieces of wood needed should be ⅛ by ½ by 10 inches.** Rather than buying or milling thin wood (the usual available size is ½ inch), consider obtaining very thin molding or wood cabinet veneer. If bamboo grows in your area or a local florist will supply you with some, the hunt for thin woods can be a short one. Very little tooling is involved in the making of the tweezers, as proven by the following tools list.

EQUIPMENT

Coping saw or a fine-toothed backsaw
Wood file
Small, smooth double-cut file
C-clamp
Waterproof white glue
Protractor
Sandpaper: grades 220, 280, 400 (aluminum oxide paper)
Steel wool: extra fine grade 0000
Soft, lint-free cloth

PROCEDURE

A glance at the illustration quickly reveals how simple the steps are. No more than an hour is required to make your first taco tweezer. Illustration A shows both top and side views of the two pieces of wood. Cut to these specifications. Before proceeding to Illustration B, sand all sides of both woods. It is more convenient at this time to do so, as sanding after they have been glued is awkward.

Once sanded, pick one end of each wood strip to be mitered for clamping. The mitering is best done with a wood file. Mitering begins 1¼ inches back from the edge of the woods (see Illustration D). The angle of the miter determines how wide the separation of the tips of the tweezers will be. I have chosen an angle of about 20 degrees. Both pieces of wood should be mitered in an identical fashion for best fit. Periodically, check to see if both pieces interface properly. A good join is necessary for optimum performance. Surface adhesion is also enhanced with a smooth and tight fit.

Before gluing and clamping the two tapered ends, ease the front tips of the tweezers with the wood file. Illustration B shows a good angle for a graceful taper. Ease all edges of the utensil with 280 and 400 sandpaper. Finish up with a few minutes of steel-wool sanding to give a shiny and glasslike finish.

Apply a small dab of waterproof glue to both surfaces of the woods that are to be joined. With your forefinger, spread the glue around to make sure the entire surface of both parts are covered. Clamp with a C-clamp, the glue will ooze from the joint, but simply wipe off with a damp cloth until no residual amount shows. If you think that indentations might be made in the clamped portion, due to the pressure exerted by the metal or wood clamps, then insert two pieces of shim stock (thin pieces of scrap wood)

to separate the metal of the clamp from the soft surface of the tweezer. Tighten. The insert will absorb the brunt of the pressure. It is quite easy to inadvertently glue the shim stock to the clamp with the excess glue that is likely to spill over. A close inspection will reveal any troublesome areas, which can then be corrected.

Let the tweezers dry overnight or for twenty-four hours before they are used. No sealing or oiling is suggested, as they are not likely to be subjected to boiling water that often. Of course, if you have other plans that do incorporate hot water, by all means, rub some vegetable oil into the wood for longer life.

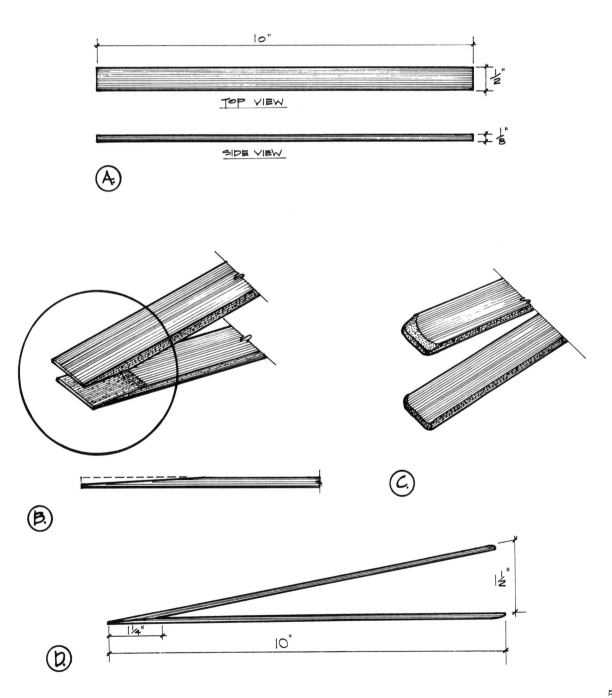

THREE SERVING PADDLES

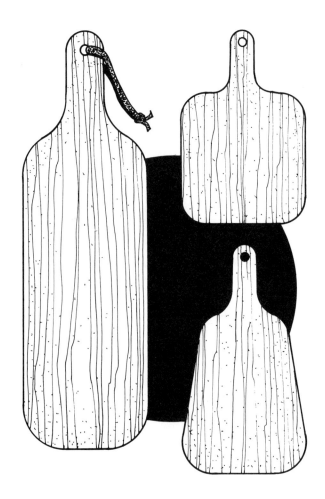

Serving paddles can be used on many occasions and for a whole host of meat and vegetable fares. Though not a common staple in the United States, the paddle form is conspicuous in many European and Near Eastern countries. It is frequently used in Japan, Korea, Formosa, China, the Philippines, Hawaii, and in many cold climate countries to deliver large tureens of stews, soups, and broths. Serving paddles make excellent cutting surfaces for sour dough bread, long loaves of French bread, and individual rolls. They are designed to withstand abuse, and the direct result is that they simply become weathered and aged in appearance which often adds to their character and form. Shapes may be round, oval, elliptical, or squared with slightly rounded corners to prevent dog-earring or fraying. Invariably composed of one piece of solid wood, the handles are designed to not only feel comfortable in the hand, but to give balance to the paddle once it is loaded with hefty servings. Pizza parlors employ paddles with handles up to 48 inches in length to place and remove platters of

pizza from deep ovens. So, experiment with different handle lengths to suit your needs.

WOOD

If you have clearly decided to use the paddle for serving only, then consider a wood with aesthetic appeal combined with hardness. Zebrawood or red oak are surefire winning choices. Grain figuration is not only for appearance, but for design consideration as well. If, on the other hand, you anticipate using the paddles as a surface upon which to cut, then perhaps a short grain, but hard wood, should be your choice. In this category oak, ash, maple, or wood of fruit-bearing trees, such as lemon, orange, or peach, make wonderfully light and durable implements.

EQUIPMENT

Coping saw
¼-inch drill bit and hand or power drill
Sandpaper: grades 120, 220, 280, 400 (aluminum oxide paper)
Steel wool: grade 400 (optional)
Pencil #2
Ruler

PROCEDURE

Experiment with shapes on paper first. The versions illustrated here are but a few possibilities based on the basic geometric shapes—the square, circle, and triangle. Use a ruler or compass to aid you in drawing shapes. Once you make a drawing to suit your sense of scale and shape, transfer the drawing to the top surface of the wood. (See Chapter 3 for instructions.) A coping saw is used to cut along the penciled line. This is usually done with one continuous cut; the angles are not too acute and the saw is designed for just this purpose.

Note the grain of the wood and that it runs from top to bottom of the paddle. This will keep the utensil strong, as a grain running perpendicular to the long shape offers weaker support to the overall tool.

A ¼-inch drill bit and drill are used to bore the centered hole in the top section of the handle. A thorough sanding, beginning with the coarser grade of paper and finishing with the aluminum oxide paper, will provide a smooth surface. For a more polished top and bottom use grade 400 steel wool. Sand in the direction of the grain. Any scratches resulting from the sandpaper can be removed with the steel wool.

Many paddles are displayed in the food preparation areas of homes in the Orient, and so, with a thin leather lash, a finishing touch becomes a functional hanging cord for the paddle. Remember too that a set of three paddles looks even better than one.

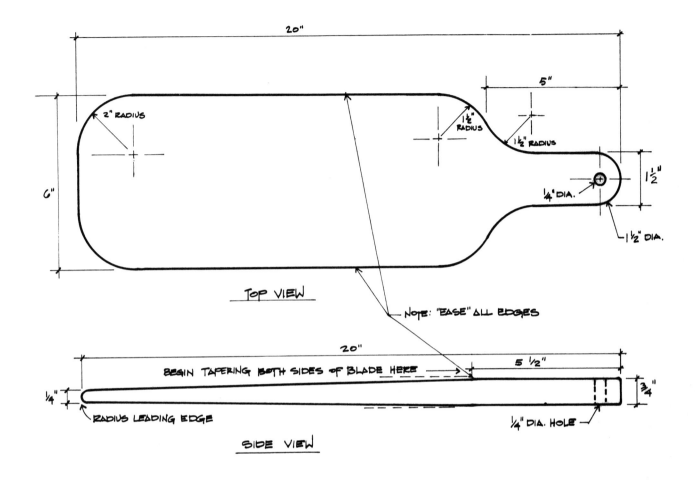

20"

2" RADIUS

6"

5"

1½" RADIUS

1½" RADIUS

1½"

¼" DIA.

1½" DIA.

TOP VIEW

NOTE: "EASE" ALL EDGES

20"

5 ½"

BEGIN TAPERING BOTH SIDES OF BLADE HERE

¼"

¾"

RADIUS LEADING EDGE

¼" DIA. HOLE

SIDE VIEW

BAMBOO CONDIMENT TRAY

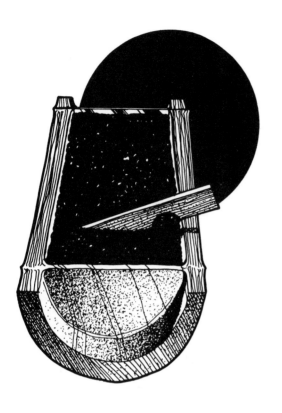

Condiment trays or dishes are used not only for basic garnishes and spices, but can also be used for more delicate offerings, such as caviar, soft cheeses, dollops of marmalade, coarse black pepper, horseradish, sturgeon, and sesame seeds. Equally simple in its shape and its function, the bamboo condiment tray will lend itself to a more natural table-side setting. One for every member of the family or guest is a thoughtful touch that will not be taken for granted or overlooked.

WOOD

Large bamboo is not easy to locate in many parts of the country. Therefore, consider smaller stems which can often be obtained from florists or raffia and caneworks stores. The West Coast abounds in many species of bamboo which can often be found growing near marshy areas, roadsides, backyards, or as cuttings from a botanical gardens. Once procured, allow the bamboo to thoroughly dry.

EQUIPMENT

Coping saw
Steel wool: grade 00
Pencil #2
Ruler
Vegetable oil (or mineral or olive oil)
Soft, lint-free cloth

PROCEDURE

Note where the rings of the bamboo form an outer raised surface. Measure ½ inch out from both the first and second node to their respective right and left ridges. It is at this point that the two saw cuts are made. Saw slowly as bamboo is made up of many fine, stringy fibrils which appear ragged when too fast a saw cut is made. Saw completely through on both cuts. Steel wool both the inside and outside of the bamboo on these outer ends. Next, with the coping saw, cut the bamboo in half lengthwise. Again, sand the inside of the bamboo to remove slight irregularities. Use a cloth dipped in ½ teaspoon of vegetable oil to lubricate the inside and remove any fine particles.

The flat applicator is a strip of flat bamboo which may be notched to gently rest on the upper rim of the tray.

Needless to say, one long bamboo stalk will provide you with more than enough trays to serve a troop of guests. Watch out! Children love this one, and it is likely that condiments will be used generously rather than gingerly, with this group, who tend to be enchanted with nontraditional tableware.

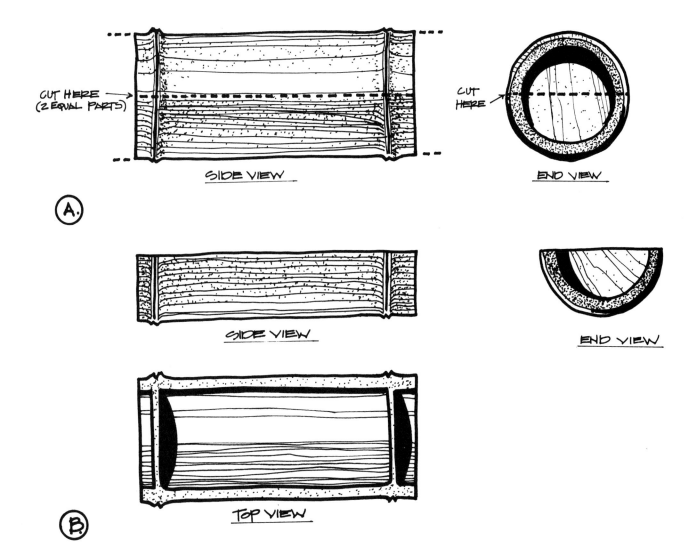

CUT HERE
(2 EQUAL PARTS)

SIDE VIEW

END VIEW

CUT
HERE

A.

SIDE VIEW

END VIEW

TOP VIEW

B.

EGG CUP

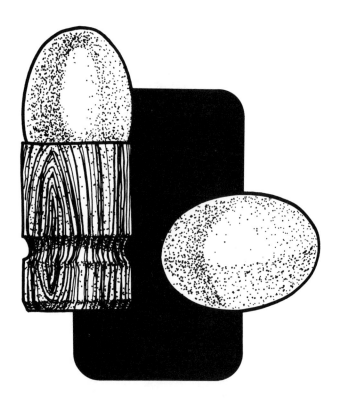

The egg cup I have used here is based on the very reliable shape of the egg itself. Consider what its most primary objectives must be. It should hold the egg firmly as it is nestled in its container with neat fit. Considering the lovely, but peculiar, shape of the egg, this is quite a feat. It should have an engaging and simple form that is capable of cheering up the grumpiest and most disheveled of break-fasters. An egg cup must keep the egg upright for the eater who uses a spoon to eat from its exposed top. Last, but not least, it must also be easy to clean. So, this mild-mannered utensil has been designed to satisfy the most grueling of tests, and is a whole lot of fun to make. One piece of wood, a few handtools, and a day's effort are, I can assure you, all you need.

WOOD

Undeniably, for its composition and appearance, beech is the ideal wood to use for this project. It is highly resistant to swelling when immersed in water, poses no problem in cleaning, and offers an easy, even material with which the woodworker should not encounter any problems. Best bets for a second choice are oak, birch, or ash. Light in color, hard in composition, these hardwoods will withstand an enormous amount of abuse, considering the workout this

implement is likely to receive after a year's use. Consider making more than one the first time. Just work the wood in stages and let the small chips fly. You will need one piece of wood, **3⅛ inches in length by 2⅛ inches in width.**

EQUIPMENT
Coping saw
Small, round wood file
Wood clamp or vise
Spoon-bit gouge
Wood mallet
Sandpaper: grades 80, 120, 220, 280, 400 (aluminum oxide paper)
Flat file
Steel wool, extra fine grade 0000
Pencil #2
Ruler

PROCEDURE
As mentioned, the egg cup is formed from one piece of wood. The diameter of the wood is 2 inches as seen in the end view of Illustration A. The overall length measures 3 inches. If you begin with square stock, you will need to file the wood to create its round shape. Gross areas of the wood are best cut away with the coping saw just prior to filing. The process is not a lengthy one, but a smooth and fully round shape is the objective of this forming process. Once the form is obtained, notch the lower portion with a small round file. This treatment will add sculptural appeal to the final product. Ease the bottom edge for a more pleasing contour. A 45-degree angle is used on the bottom ⅛ inch for best results.

The next step is to lock the round stock in a clamp or vise in such a way that the top portion is accessible to the carving tool. With short and light taps on the mallet and spoon-bit gouge, carve the inside of the cup to gradually form the scooped shape that will eventually cradle the egg. Continue to carve to a depth of 1¾ inches. As you progress, use a hard-boiled egg to test for proper fit. Highlights or lumps still in the wood are marked with a pencil and then cut away with the mallet and gouge until a relatively even surface is obtained. Sanding the inside with 80 sandpaper will smoothen the roughest of spots. The outside of the cup is sanded with 120 paper to begin with. The finer grades are used both on the inside and outside in progressive stages.

Be sure to rotate the stock as you carve. The gouge is much easier to work when the woodworker has adopted an angle that is approximately at 45 degrees to the interior bowl of the cup.

Finish sanding with grade 400 paper. Use grade 0000 steel wool to give the egg cup its smoothest finish.

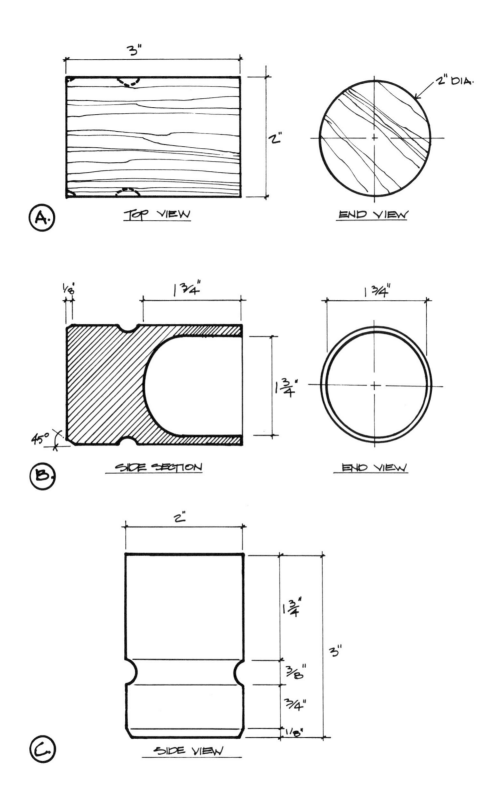

3"

2"

2" DIA.

A. TOP VIEW   END VIEW

1/8"   1 3/4"   1 3/4"

1 3/4"

45°

B. SIDE SECTION   END VIEW

2"

1 3/4"

3/8"   3"

3/4"

1/8"

C. SIDE VIEW

OAK SERVING TRAY

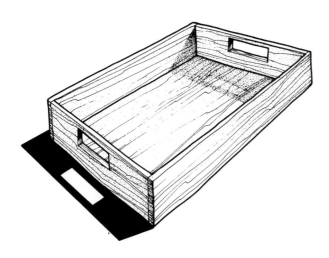

Here is a tray that is elegant enough for serving cordials to visiting royalty and durable enough to hastily bus dishes from the dining table or buffet. Fitted with two windows that serve as openings to conveniently carry the tray, this design is made all the more attractive by the right tones of red or yellow oak. It is simply constructed by means of butt joints and can be breezily made within a few hours. Use it to hold your handcrafted tureens or simply hang it on the wall of your kitchen. In this time of clean Scandanavian design, when extraneous details detract from honest wood expression, this serving tray makes a most welcome debut. So, clear the decks and ready yourself for a very gratifying woodworking project.

WOOD

Oak of any color makes for a good beginning. Five pieces are required. You will need **two 12- by 4- by ½-inch strips for the short side, two 19- by 4- by ½-inch strips for the long side, and one 18- by 12- by ½-inch panel to serve as the bottom panel.** A word about this last piece is in order here. Wood, especially good hardwood, is often difficult to find in wider dimensions. Therefore, let me suggest that you consider a laminated wood that has an oak veneer on both sides. The difference will never be detected once the tray has been constructed, and will save you the aggravation of a long search. Most lumberyards stock this material for customers in the cabinetmaking business. Therefore its availability is rarely a problem.

EQUIPMENT

Crosscut saw
Keyhole saw
Flat wood file
½-inch drill bit and hand or power drill
Large wood clamps or pipe clamps
Waterproof white glue
Soft, lint-free cloth
Cardboard applicators to apply and spread glue
Sandpaper: grades 120, 220, 280, 400 (aluminum oxide paper)
Steel wool: extra fine grade 000
Varithane Semi-Matte Finish-Sealer (Varithane is a brand name)
Paintbrush
Pencil #2
Ruler

PROCEDURE

Measure, mark, and cut all panels to the prescribed sizes. A preliminary sanding with grades 120 and 220 sandpaper is done at this point while the panels are more easily worked. Sand with the grain.

Mark the four corners of each window. With the ½-inch drill bit, bore a hole in each respective corner. With the keyhole saw, cut straight lines from one hole to the next to, in effect, cut out a square window. The four corners, which are now rounded as a result of the drill, are lightly filed flat to form a clean 90-degree angle on all four corners. Repeat this procedure on the second panel.

Lay all five pieces of wood on the worktable, with each panel positioned according to its assembly. The tray can be compared to a thick, but shallow, shoe box, and it is this modified shape that the tray will take.

Apply a thin bead of glue to the lower portions of the two short panels and clamp to the bottom panel. Wipe away the oozing glue with a damp rag. Allow to stand for twenty-four hours. Once dry, install the two remaining panels, which also have been glued, and once again clamp to the other panels. Allow to dry.

Rough or uneven edges are sanded until a good right angle is achieved. Marred edges are unsightly and should be worked over until all edges are perpendicular to the bottom of the tray.

Sand all surfaces, including the underside of the tray, and finish sanding with fine steel wool. Use the tack rag to remove all traces of sawdust, powder, sandpaper grit, and steel wool.

With a good, clean brush, apply a thin coat of Varithane Sealer to all surfaces of the tray. Follow manufacturer's directions for drying conditions and length of time. Apply a second and third coat if necessary. Lightly steel wool in between each coat. As usual, use the tack rag to ensure a clean surface.

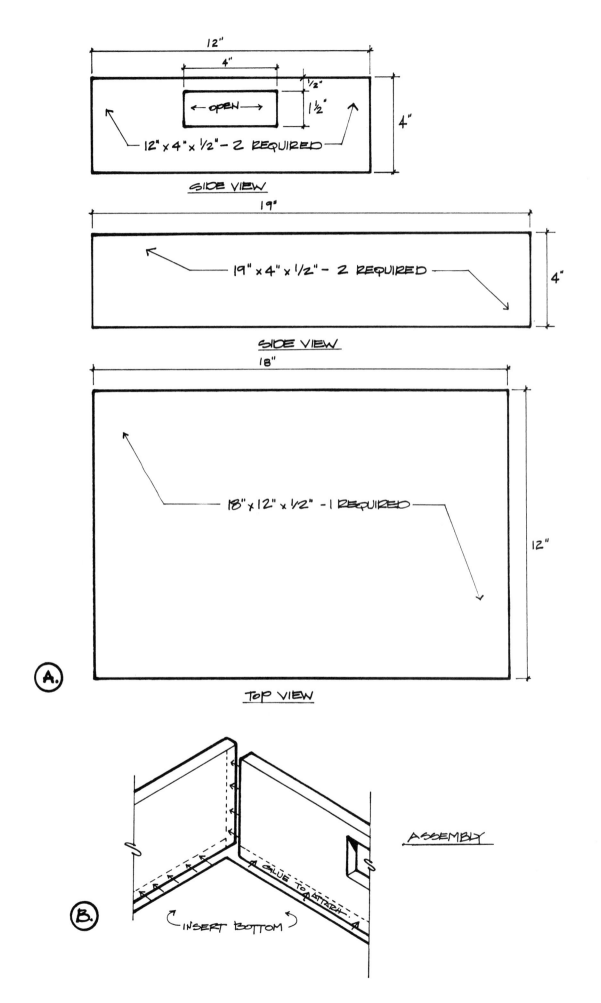

12"

4"

← OPEN →

½"

1½"

4"

12" x 4" x ½" - 2 REQUIRED

SIDE VIEW

19"

4"

19" x 4" x ½" - 2 REQUIRED

SIDE VIEW

18"

12"

18" x 12" x ½" - 1 REQUIRED

Ⓐ.

TOP VIEW

Ⓑ.

ASSEMBLY

GLUE TO ATTACH

(INSERT BOTTOM)

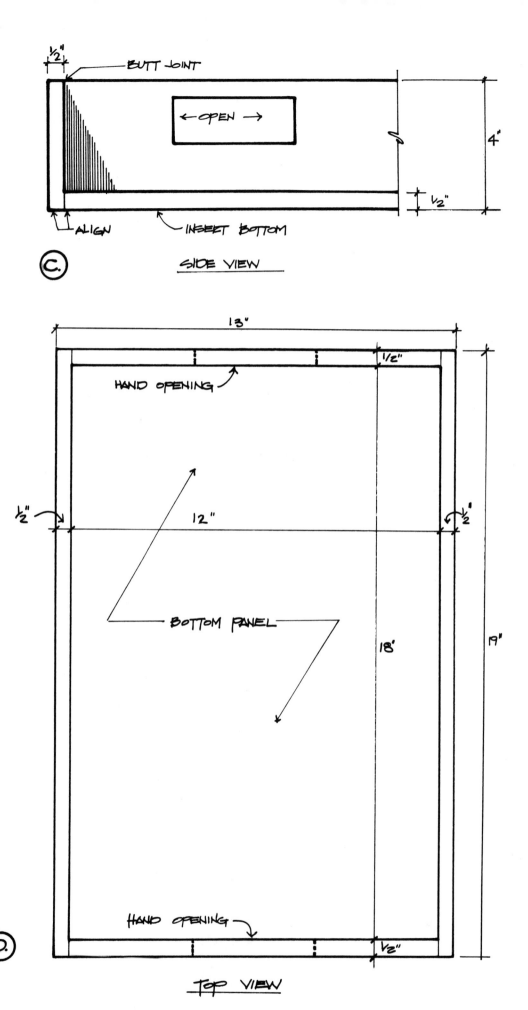

½"

BUTT JOINT

← OPEN →

4"

½"

ALIGN

INSERT BOTTOM

C. SIDE VIEW

13"

½"

HAND OPENING

½"

12"

½"

BOTTOM PANEL

18'

19"

HAND OPENING

½"

D. TOP VIEW

SMALL CONDIMENT JAR AND SPOON

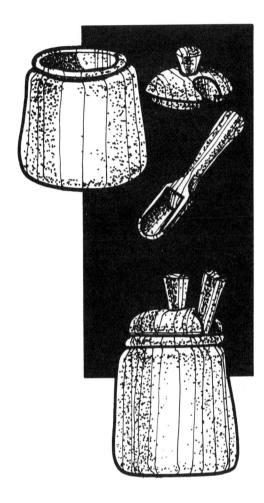

Here is the perfect condiment container to keep tableside for those wishing a bit of this or a dash of that. A sculptural little gem, this project requires a little more skill than the preceding two examples, but, by now, if you have made the others, this one won't prove too hard. You are a veteran at this point, and by reviewing the working procedures for those projects you will be well on your way.

There are four parts to this project—the bottle, the lid, the lid's handle (plug), and the small serving spoon. Each is formed according to the illustrations, which have been carefully rendered to simplify and clarify any potentially confusing steps.

WOOD

Because of the intricacy of the project, a softwood is best for the first attempt. If you like the results consider a harder and more decorative wood the next time. For the bottle you will need a square block **2¼ by 2 by 2 inches.** The rest of the requirements are as follows: **lid, ½ by 1¾ inches; plug, ⅜ by ⅜ inch; spoon, 2 by ½ by ½ inch.**

EQUIPMENT

Coping saw
C-clamp or table vise
1½-inch drill bit or drill bit accessory, ⅜-inch drill bit, and hand or power drill
Flat wood file
Rattail wood file
Animal hide glue
Wood-carving knife (pocket knife) with sharp blade
Sandpaper: grades 120, 220, 280, 400 (aluminum oxide paper)
Steel wool: grade 00
Pencil #2
Ruler

PROCEDURE

Locate the center of your block of wood by means of two diagonal lines that intersect in the middle of the top plain of the block. Drill a 1½-inch wide hole in the block to a depth of 2 inches. Remove the block from the vise or clamp and proceed to saw by means of the coping saw to form a round cylinder. Notch the upper portion of the jar with the rattail file.

The lid is carved to fit the inner diameter of the jar and is done gradually to ensure a snug fit. A ¼-inch hole is drilled in the center of the lid which will soon accommodate the small handle. The hole need not travel through the lid. A depth of ¼ inch is adequate. Apply a small drop of glue to the just-drilled hole and insert the small handle which can be best obtained from a ¼-inch dowel rod. Sand the top of the handle to round the edge a bit. The handle must be allowed to sit until the glue has had sufficient time to dry.

The spoon is carved from a 2-inch strip of ½-inch dowel with the knife and is designed to fit inside the jar while the top of the handle protrudes from the lid.

Once the handle of the spoon has been completed, measure the diameter on the uppermost portion. It is this measurement that must now be cut away on the jar's lid in order to accommodate the handle. Consult Illustration C, top view.

Sand all pieces with the recommended grades of sandpaper.

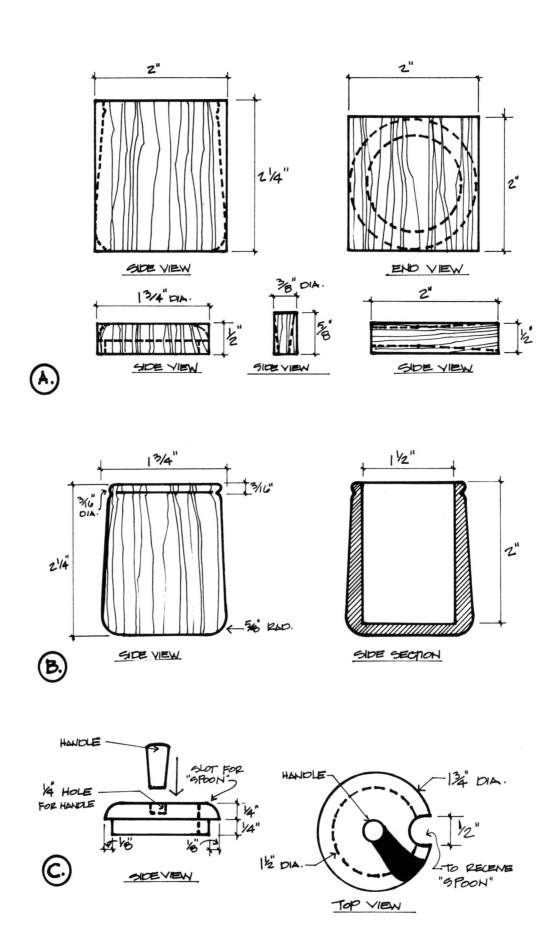

2"

2 1/4"

SIDE VIEW

2"

2"

END VIEW

1 3/4" DIA.

1/2"

SIDE VIEW

3/8" DIA.

5/8"

SIDE VIEW

2"

1/2"

SIDE VIEW

A.

1 3/4"

3/16"

3/16" DIA.

2 1/4"

5/8" RAD.

SIDE VIEW

1 1/2"

2"

SIDE SECTION

B.

HANDLE

SLOT FOR "SPOON"

1/4" HOLE FOR HANDLE

1/4"

1/4"

1/8"

1/8"

SIDE VIEW

HANDLE

1 3/4" DIA.

1/2"

1 1/2" DIA.

TO RECEIVE "SPOON"

TOP VIEW

C.

62

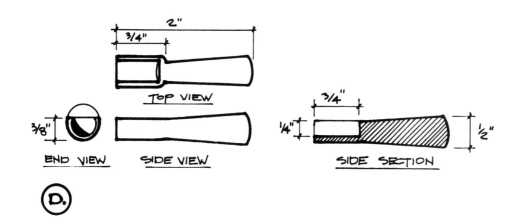

2"

3/4"

TOP VIEW

3/8"

END VIEW   SIDE VIEW

3/4"

1/4"   1/2"

SIDE SECTION

Ⓓ.

SIDE VIEW

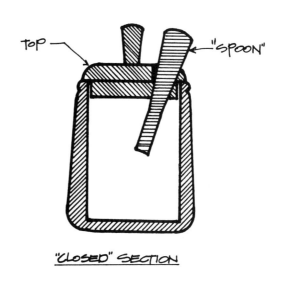

TOP   "SPOON"

"CLOSED" SECTION

Ⓔ.

WOOD TRIVET

Use this wood trivet on the dining room table or in the microwave oven. Made of all wooden parts, the trivet will keep hot dishes off precious surfaces, such as hardwood tables, counters, and plastic countertops. The cook who finds microwave heating an added convenience in the kitchen will discover that food is more quickly heated when placed on this trivet, since the dish is raised from the oven's surface which allows for greater exposure. Microwave ovens are designed with a plastic interior which can be scratched if too hard a tray or dish is roughly seated in the oven's interior. The wood trivet will decrease the likelihood of this occurring, since a softwood is recommended for its composition.

WOOD
Pine is an excellent choice. It is cheap, easy to work, and is readily available. To fasten the top ribs of wood to the frame use small ⅛-inch wood dowel pegs. You will need thirty-four ⅛-inch pegs, each ⅜ inch in length. The ribs, of which there are seventeen, measure ¼ by ¼ by 8½ inches. The two side rails, which are used to support the rails and

work as a frame, **measure ¾ by ¼ by 10⅝ inches.** Insist on straight wood stock if you buy from a lumberyard. The wood is also to be free of knots, cracks, oozing sap fissures, and other flaws. Kiln-dried wood is ideal and is still quite affordable. White pine, yellow pine, sugar pine, and other varieties are equally useful.

EQUIPMENT
Backsaw
⅛-inch drill bit and hand or power drill
Waterproof white glue
Soft-head mallet (leather or hard rubber)
Wood clamps or C-clamps
Sandpaper: grades 220, 280, 400 (aluminum oxide paper)
Pencil #2
Ruler

PROCEDURE
Illustrations A, B, and C are quite specific with respect to the overall plan of how the materials are to be spaced. All measurements have been accurately detailed and indicated for you. Illustration C should be studied first to ascertain the overall look and configuration of the trivet. Then look over the measurements in the other two drawings.

With a pencil and ruler, measure out all pieces of stock and carefully mark for cutting. The backsaw is used to cut the wood and is a good all-around saw for more detailed pieces. Once all the components have been cut, separate the woods into three groups — two rails, thirty-four peg dowels, seventeen rails. By means of a straight ruler, as opposed to a tape measure, indicate where all holes are to be drilled with the hand drill and ⅛-inch bit. All holes are drilled ⅝ inch on center, as shown in Illustration B.

Assemble the woods by placing the two rails parallel to one another, and then proceed to lightly glue the holes in both rails. Lay the topmost rail first, the bottommost rail, second. This will help to stablize the frame. Continue to assemble each rib until all seventeen are neatly seated. The pegs may require the help of the soft-head mallet, which is used to lightly tap the pegs until they lie flush to the top surface. When drilling holes use the clamps to hold the wood firmly in its place. Drill holes at exact 90-degree angles to the wood's surface to ensure even rows. This will also minimize the possibility of the pegs going in at awkward angles.

Lightly sand all pieces before they are installed, or you may sand once the trivet has been completed, if you prefer.

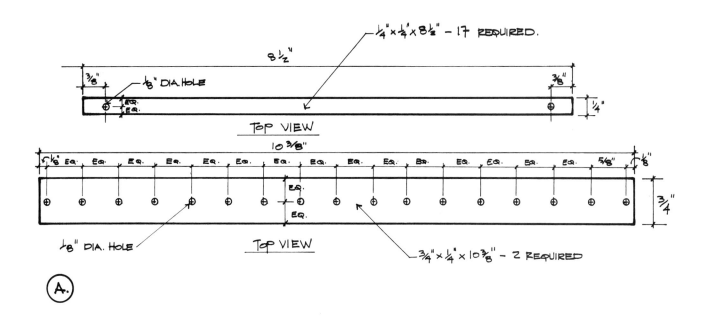

$\frac{1}{4}" \times \frac{1}{4}" \times 8\frac{1}{2}"$ – 17 REQUIRED.

$8\frac{1}{2}"$

$\frac{3}{8}"$ $\frac{1}{8}"$ DIA. HOLE $\frac{3}{8}"$ $\frac{1}{4}"$

EQ.
EQ.

TOP VIEW

$10\frac{3}{8}"$

$\frac{1}{8}"$ EQ. EQ. EQ. EQ. EQ. EQ. EQ. EQ. EQ. EQ. EQ. EQ. EQ. EQ. $\frac{5}{8}"$ $\frac{1}{8}"$

EQ.
EQ.

$\frac{3}{4}"$

$\frac{1}{8}"$ DIA. HOLE

TOP VIEW

$\frac{3}{4}" \times \frac{1}{4}" \times 10\frac{3}{8}"$ – 2 REQUIRED

(A.)

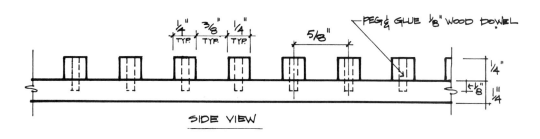

$\frac{1}{4}"$ TYP. $\frac{3}{8}"$ TYP. $\frac{1}{4}"$ TYP.

$\frac{5}{8}"$

PEG & GLUE $\frac{1}{8}"$ WOOD DOWEL

$\frac{1}{4}"$

$\frac{1}{8}"$ $\frac{1}{4}"$

SIDE VIEW

(B)

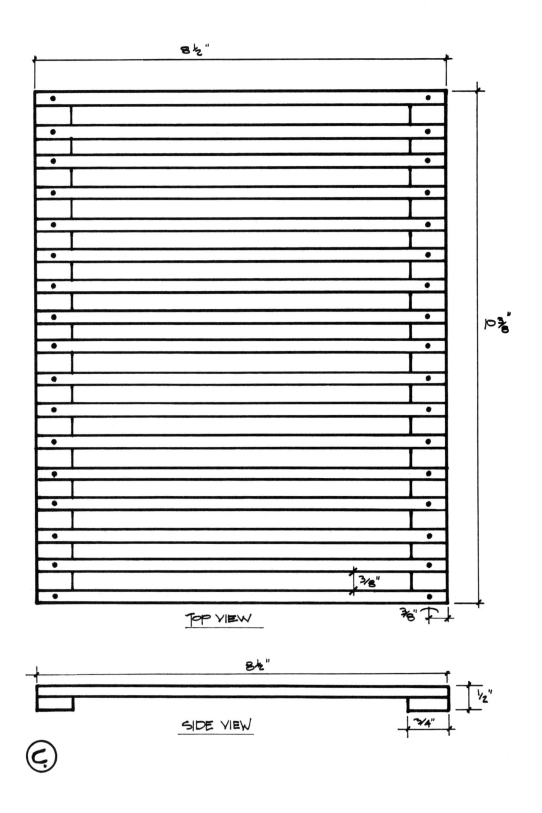

8½"

10⅜"

3/8"

3/8"

TOP VIEW

8½"

½"

¼"

SIDE VIEW

C.

66

SALAD TONGS

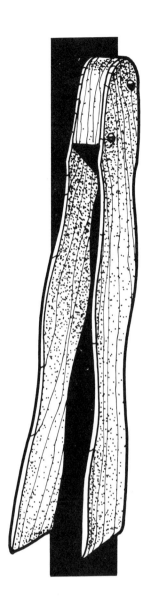

Shredded food is often difficult to handle and this well-designed and striking implement works like a charm for those who like to get "close in" with salads, julienne strips of ham, carrot strings, and Armenian string cheese. Around our house, we keep a set of these tongs within reach to remove hot dogs from boiling water, and on occasion, they double as grips for pulling out scorching-hot oven grates. (The oven mitt invariably gets tucked away under dish towels on the other side of the kitchen.) These salad tongs work by simple compression, provide a mean grip, and are a breeze to clean. No gluing is necessary and the finished utensil looks poised and in keeping with the rest of your growing gallery of wooden kitchen utensils and accessories.

WOOD

Three pieces of hardwood and four brads make up this device. **The two arms measure 9 inches in overall length and 1 inch in width. The wooden wedge, which separates the arms, measures ¾ inch at its peak and tapers to ½ inch. The wedge is simply a small block of wood, measuring ¾ inch high by 1 inch in width by 1 inch in length. The four brads are brass and measure ⅜ inch in length.** If you plan to set these tongs table-side, why not consider a more exotic species of wood, such as walnut or mahogany, or wood with a pronounced figure, such as elm of the burled type, padouk, or rosewood? Zebrawood should not be over-looked for its contrasting colors and grain accents. Of course, the lighter hardwoods, such as beech, ash, oak, or maple, work nicely, too.

Don't let the hardness of the wood be a deterrent in your choice. As with most of the smaller projects in this book, the tongs are made with simple hand tools that allow you more control and permit a more leisurely rhythm of working to match your pace.

EQUIPMENT

Coping saw
C-clamp or table vise
Smooth wood file
Light hammer
Sandpaper: grades 120, 200, 280, 400 (aluminum oxide paper)
Steel wool: extra fine grade 0000
Pencil #2
Ruler
Vegetable oil (or mineral or olive oil)
Soft, lint-free cloth

PROCEDURE

I have avoided specifying the thickness of the two 9- by 1-inch arms in order to accommodate several choices you have, which largely depend on the availability of the thinner woods. Ideally, for lightness and strength, something in the neighborhood of ⅛ to ³/₁₆ inch would be most adequate. Most likely, these thinner woods fall into the category of veneers and thin molding used for cabinet and other woodworking trim. Once again, bamboo makes for a neat solution to this problem, should it be within reach.

The top view in Illustration A maps out the overall proportion and configuration of the salad tongs. On tracing paper, trace the rectangle first. Then, with a thin line, draw in the contour of the soon-to-be-cut arm. The same pattern will work for both arms. Transfer the drawing to the two pieces of wood, making sure that the drawings are symmetrical; i.e., one is the mirror image of the other. (For tracing and transferring instructions see Chapter 3).

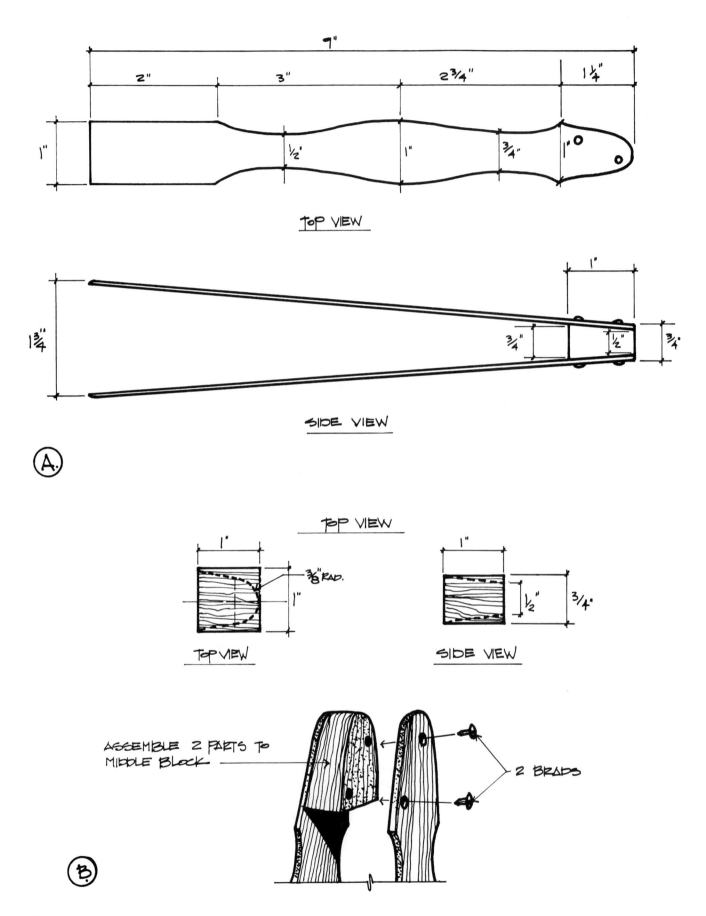

9"

2"   3"   2¾"   1¼"

1"

½"   1"   ¾"   1"

TOP VIEW

1¾"

1"

¾"

½"

¾"

SIDE VIEW

(A.)

TOP VIEW

1"

⅜" RAD.

1"

TOP VIEW

1"

½"

¾"

SIDE VIEW

ASSEMBLE 2 PARTS TO MIDDLE BLOCK

2 BRADS

(B.)

Clamp with a C-clamp, or tighten the wood in a vise, and proceed to cut along the wavy line until the entire shape is free from the wood. Repeat this step once again for the other arm. The width of the ends should be ⅜ inch. The block will need to be shaped to this specification for an integrated fit. At this time, sand both arms. Start with the coarse sandpaper and work your way through the rest of the papers, finishing off with the steel wool (follow the order given in the equipment list). Ease all edges and slightly taper the front tips of the two arms with the smooth wood file.

The block wedge, which serves as the fulcrum, is drawn and cut to fit between the two back ends of the arms. Any irregularity in the shape can be filed with the smooth wood file to enable it to conform to the shape of the arms. Both faces of the wedge are to be flat. Sand the block using the same grades of paper as before.

With two brass brads set on a bias to one another (i.e., upper right and lower left), gently tap one arm into the wedge with a light tacking hammer. It is not necessary to countersink the nails; the brass makes an attractive accent. Place the flat side of the just-filed arm face down on the work surface, position the second arm in the identical way, and tap in the remaining two brads. Squeeze the tongs a few times to determine if the brads stay seated.

Lubricate the tongs with a small amount of vegetable oil by vigorously rubbing with a dry lint-free cloth. If the tongs are used frequently, an occasional polish with the oil will extend the life of the wood. Hardened food particles can be loosened and removed by allowing the tongs to soak for fifteen to twenty minutes in hot, soapy water. Stubborn particles are removed with a plastic scouring pad. Expect discoloration on light woods. They will soon take on a well-seasoned look.

SPATULA AND BREAD KNIFE

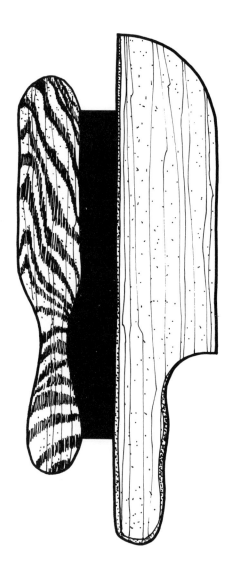

Here are two utensils that will be put to excellent use in your kitchen. The spreading spatula (on the left in illustration) is a best bet for applying and smoothing cake icings, sugar-coated hot cross buns, and even peanut butter with one pass! Easy to make, even easier to clean, the unpretentious blade performs a host of functions and will be part of your stable of oft-used cooking tools. The bread knife (right) which resembles a meat cleaver, is a fanciful serving knife for cakes, breads, pies, quiches, chocolate mousses, casseroles, or any food that must be divided into smaller portions. Use it to cut bread at the dinner table, rather than to dice, shred, or chop in the kitchen, jobs for which its metal counterpart is far better equipped.

Both utensils are made from one piece of wood, thereby eliminating the need to fit handle to blade. The proportions may vary according to your personal requirements and the utensils can be fabricated in an assortment of sizes. Both utensils are indispensable for such cooking preliminaries as dough stirring, flapjack turning, or even fine cream sauce stirring. It would seem as if every kitchen activity is represented in these implements.

WOOD AND OTHER MATERIALS

I used two different types of wood for the spatula and knife. The spatula is composed of zebrawood, rather hard-to-find, but extremely attractive, hardwood. The knife is of ash, a rather common wood found in lumberyards or in the scrap bins of local cabinetmakers. Needless to say, neither wood choice is essential to the tools' continued usefulness, but, since I was keenly interested in giving both implements a sharp edge by means of a pronounced taper to the edges, and too fine an edge would wear down after several days of the usual cooking activity, I chose two hardwoods known for their strength, close grain, and overall appearance to obviate the problem of premature dulling. The utensils must be well balanced to perform those extra heavy-duty assignments, where flipping, folding, etc. are required. To accomplish this, larger utensils than the ones pictured here should be attempted.

Other choices for wood might be maple, beech, basswood, hickory, or chestnut. Since no nailing or fitting of parts is required, the hardness of the wood should pose no problem. Sizes of wood can vary. **Start with a piece of wood measuring 10½ inches in length, 1⅝ inches wide, and ⅝ inch thick.**

If you intend to hang your tool, you will need a **thin piece of leather about 5 inches long.**

EQUIPMENT

Coping saw
C-clamp or table vise
Surform flat file or smooth wood file
Sandpaper: grades 120, 220, 280, 400 (aluminum oxide paper)
Steel wool: extra fine grade 000
Vegetable oil (or olive or mineral oil)
Soft, lint-free cloth
Pencil #2
Ruler
⅜-inch drill bit and hand or power drill (*optional*)
Thin strip of leather, 5 inches long

PROCEDURE FOR SPATULA

The spatula's overall length measures 10 inches exactly. It is 1½ inches wide and ¼ inch thick. These dimensions are for the wood prior to the shaping, i.e., raw stock. Since I feel that as little waste as possible is best, you will note that the tolerances are not great. It then behooves you to work in a Spartan manner.

The spatula is symmetrical and is best planned on paper as follows: Fold a piece of 10-inch-long paper and draw one side of the spatula on it, following the illustration. Cut along the contour line through both layers of paper with scissors, and then unfold the paper to reveal the full design, much like a paper doll cutout. Using the transfer technique given in Chapter 3, transpose the drawing to the top side of the wood's surface. A drawing is unnecessary for the utensil's edge.

With the coping saw, cut away the outline of the tool, making sure to maintain the graceful contour of the utensil's overall shape, as suggested by the drawn line.

With the flat wood file or the Surform wood file, lightly stroke the edge of the spatula's edge. The effect should be one of slightly tapering all the way around. The taper begins about ½ inch in from the utensil's edge. The same degree of taper is maintained for a uniform shape. Periodically, run your fingers over the edge to check for uniform sharpness and consistency of angle. The objective is not to make a knife's edge by honing it so sharp that it is likely to splinter, but to make an edge that will effortlessly slide under foods on tin, glass, or other cooking and serving surfaces. The handle's neck and the handle itself, starting 5⅜ inches back from the nose of the spatula, constitute the remainder of the utensil. The handle is uniform in thickness and all edges are to be eased for a comfortable feel and fit. Drill a ⅜-inch hole where indicated, if the tool is to be strung with the leather thong. Sand with coarse sandpaper, working through the finer grades. Finish with steel wool. Rub vegetable oil into wood to seal pores.

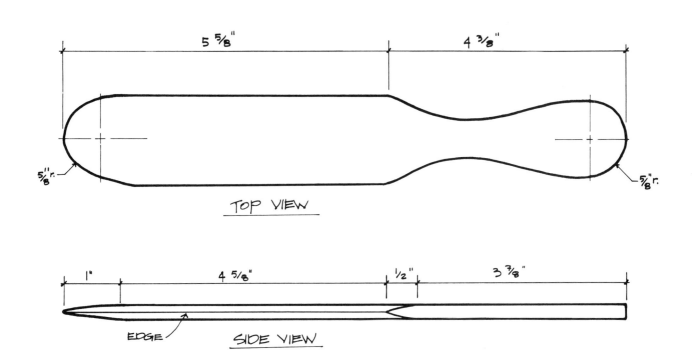

5 ⅝"   4 ⅜"

⅝" r.   ⅝" r.

TOP VIEW

1"   4 ⅝"   ½"   3 ⅜"

EDGE   SIDE VIEW

PROCEDURE FOR THE BREAD KNIFE

After tracing the pattern, transfer the knife's outline to the flat side of the block of wood, and proceed to cut with the coping saw. (If you want your knife to be a different size than what is shown in the illustration, determine the overall dimension by working out your plans with paper and pencil, considering balance, fit, storage, etc. After a few thumbnail sketches have been completed, make a master drawing on tracing paper and continue.) The entire top of the knife is one straight edge. Only the ends are curved to form the butt of the handle and the sweep of the cutting edge. Note the slight hump in the lower grip of the handle. This will enable you to have a firm grip as you slice. With the wood file or the Surform file, file the cutting edge, starting 2 inches back from the edge. Ease all edges by means of the coarse sandpaper (120), and work through the smoother grades, finally finishing off the sanding activity with steel wool to give the smoothest of finishes.

Use one of the natural oils to give a rich finish and let the knife stand for a day or so for maximum penetration.

Should your knife need sharpening, simply clamp in a vise or by means of a C-clamp, and, with the file, give the knife's edge a few passes to restore its original sharpness.

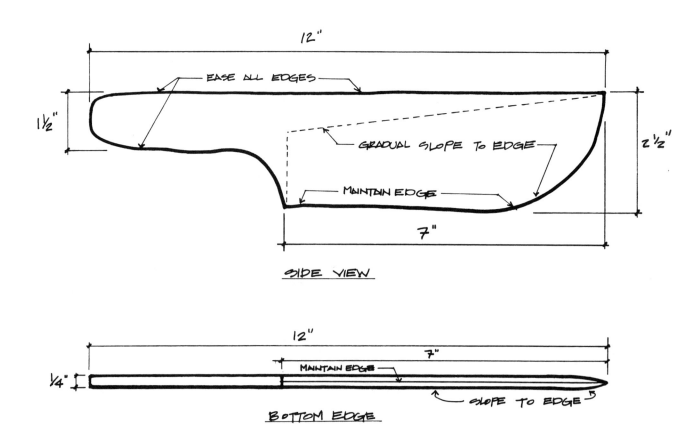

6.
Cooking Aids

KITCHEN MALLET

Hammer away on the toughest of meats with this hefty kitchen wizard. Made easily with two pieces of wood, it is less trouble than changing butchers. The no-nonsense cubical head measures approximately 2¼ inches square and balances perfectly in any cook's hand. Attractive and tough, this tool may even be used as an ice crusher. It makes meat tenderizing a breeze and lends a characteristic charm to any kitchen. Don't treat it gingerly; give it the workout it requires as you turn tough meat into tender patties for hamburgers and other meat recipes.

WOOD

Several choices of wood come to mind for this project. Oak is wonderfully durable, has interesting wood figuration, and is light in color. Beech has a simpler appearance, but can be equally hard in composition. Other hardwoods, such as maple and hickory, provide heft and resistance and

can be worked with sharp tools. Whatever wood you are scouting, remember that the principle use of the hammer is to break down the tough connective tissues in meat with gusto short of brute force. Therefore, a hammer such as this need be composed of very hard wood.

For the 11-inch handle, you might just be limited to what round woods are on hand. Hardwood dowels, are ideal, but the selection is limited, unless you can turn your own on a lathe or rescue a small leg from an abandoned hardwood table. I have designed the illustrated version with a conventional dowel handle. You may want to find a similar turned piece and join it to the hammer head. A contrasting wood color, to give a light and dark effect, could very well provide you with a beautiful, yet simple, example of the woodworker's art. **The hammer head will measure 2 by 2 by 2½ inches. The handle will measure 11 by ¾ inch.**

EQUIPMENT

Sharp cross-cut saw or backsaw (or table saw)
C-clamp or table vise
¾-inch drill bit and hand or power drill
Wooden mallet
Epoxy, cellulose, glue or Three Ton Brand Acrylic Glue
   (glues must be waterproof and nontoxic)
Sandpaper: grades 120, 220, 280, 400 (aluminum oxide
   paper)
Graph paper
Pencil #2
Ruler

PROCEDURE

The kitchen mallet is made in two parts. Begin with the head. Once the head is near completion, the handle is then made and fitted to the head.

The head requires careful drawing with a ruler and pencil and cutting to achieve the even rows of studs. Notched sides tenderize tough meat, while smooth ones slap it flat.

To achieve the knobbed facets on opposing surfaces of the hammer head, you will need a very sharp cross-cut saw. A small table saw capable of making 45-degree cuts is ideal. Whether by handsaw or power saw, the angled cuts must be carefully executed to achieve the raised pattern, as depicted in Illustration A.

Start with a 2-inch wide by 2-inch high by 2½-inch deep block of any recommended hardwood. All sides of the block are initially flat, and the block is perfectly cubical in shape. The two 2- by 2-inch sides are marked with a pencil for cutting. On graph paper, within a 2-inch square, draw thirty-six equal smaller squares, as shown in Illustration A, front view. In each of the thirty-six squares, draw two diagonal lines, which in effect, create an X or center point. These become the raised tips of the individual studs. The graph paper will help you keep lines consistent and evenly spaced. Using the pattern transfer technique described in Chapter 3, transfer the drawing to each of the two designated sides of the mallet head. If you manually saw both surfaces, then the stock should be firmly clamped to the worktable with the soon-to-be-cut surface facing upwards. Carefully angle the saw blade to make a 45-degree cut, and proceed to cut to a depth of $\frac{3}{16}$ inch. Repeat the cut in parallel fashion, until all five cuts are completed. Return to

the first cut, this time, angling the blade to the opposite 45-degree angle, and proceed to make five more cuts. The result will be six rows of ridged surfaces. If the cuts have been carefully executed, you will have cut out V-shaped strips of wood waste. Loosen the stock, rotate 90 degrees, and repeat the two steps for the other side of the mallet. Again, strips of wood should fall away, as a result, leaving a small faceted surface. If you plan to use a table saw rather than a handsaw as described, adjust the blade to 45 degrees, and, with the aid of a push stick (a piece of wood long enough to eliminate any possibility of jeopardizing hands

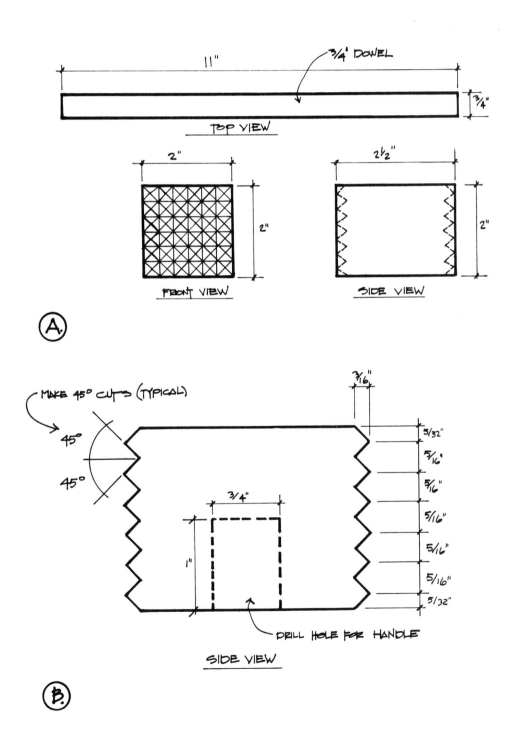

with the spinning blade), gently guide the block along the fence of the table saw and make the above cuts. Then, after examination of the cuts, repeat the entire procedure on the opposing side of the block. Uneven rows can easily be filed with a thin, smooth wood file or jeweler's file to improve cuts that are slightly askew.

On the underside of the block, locate the center point, and, with a ¾-inch drill bit or drill bit attachment, bore a hole to a depth of 1 inch.

The handle is ¾-inch diameter wood and is round in shape. The 11-inch length has proven to be about the right length for best balance. Before gluing, insert one end of the dowel in the hole of the mallet head. A tight fit, short of having to force the fit, is desirable. A tight fit can be helped along by means of lightly tapping the dowel end with a soft mallet. In either event, before fitting handle to head, apply a small amount of one of the recommended glues to the hole. Insert the handle to its fullest extent. Any glue issuing from the join should be wiped off with a damp rag. Allow overnight drying or follow manufacturer's directions for proper curing of glue and wood.

Sand handle and smooth sides of the mallet head. A little carving on the handle can be a decorative touch, adding a gentle embellishment.

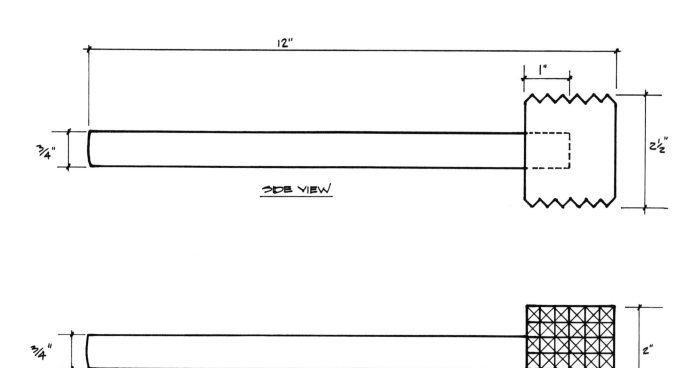

DOUGH WHEEL

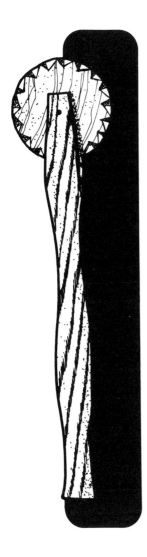

You don't have to be a big wheel to make dough with this wonderfully useful gadget. Often referred to as "pastry jiggers" or "crimpers," and historically made from whalebone or cast brass, the dough wheel is used to apply decorative scallops around the edges of pies, Quiches Lorraine, and fanciful cookies for any occasion. This pastry wheel gives a neat crimped edge, especially to lattice strips, and is also helpful for trimming ravioli. It is a real dynamo for all sorts of free-wheeling cuts—around the edge of the pie pan or just simply on the breadboard—it performs its duty well.

WOOD AND OTHER MATERIALS

The cutting wheel's edge must be sharp. When it becomes worn, it will be necessary to replace it with an identical wheel, so in order to preserve the original edge, it is wise to select a very hard wood, such as maple or hickory. If available, pear or boxwood are ideal. Oak or ash are good stand-ins and are readily available. The use of a blonde wood for the handle is a natural choice, but I have made several dough cutters with very dark woods, such as padouk, ebony, and black walnut. They get the compliments, because one can see the utilitarian function of the tool, and the contrasting woods make them stand out in any kitchen. Occasionally, they work as pizza cutters, everyone having their own to cut small or large portions.

You will need a 2- by 2-by ⅛-inch piece of hardwood for the wheel. The handle is a full 7¾-inches long by ¾-inch thick dowel rod or flat strip of hardwood.

EQUIPMENT
Coping saw
Backsaw
C-clamp or table vise
Wood-carving knife (pocket knife) with sharp blade, or
    X-acto knife with #11 blade
¼-inch drill bit and hand or power drill
½-inch-long brass nail (round head)
Sandpaper: grades 120, 220, 280, 400 (aluminum oxide
    paper)
Pencil #2
Ruler
Circle compass with lead
Brass brad

PROCEDURE
On a piece of paper, draw a 7¾- by ¾-inch rectangle. This is the measurement to be transferred to the flat wood strip that is to serve as a handle for the wheel. The circle compass is used to draw a 2-inch-diameter circle on a piece of paper. This measurement will be transferred to the block of wood (See Chapter 3) that will serve as the wheel portion of the utensil. After both drawings have been transferred to the respective woods, make preparations to cut the cutting wheel.

The square block is best cut by simply placing it in a vise or by clamping it to a table with some overhang and then proceeding to cut a 2-inch-diameter circle from the square wood. Once cut, the 360-degree circumference is then notched by means of a sharp knife by cutting into the wood at 45-degree angles. Each cut is alternated: 45-degree angle to the left, 45-degree angle to the right. One notch with two angled cuts measures about ¼ inch in typical width. The notching process is continued until the full rim is completed. With a ⅛-inch drill bit, bore a hole in the center of the wheel, being careful to make a slow exit on the opposite side of the wheel with the drill. Illustration B shows the position of the notches and center of the wheel for drilling.

The handle is cut with a coping saw, according to the proportions shown in Illustration C, top view. A $3/16$-inch-wide slot that is $1\frac{1}{2}$ inches deep must be cut to hold the wheel. This is best done with the backsaw. One cut with the saw is likely to be inadequate, since most saw blades are considerably thinner. Two additional cuts, to the right and left of the center cut, will produce a $3/16$-inch-wide channel. Examine the opening. If the wood has uneven walls or burrs, then, by means of 120 grade sandpaper, lightly work the paper back and forth to remove unwanted waves or burred surfaces. In order for the wheel to revolve freely, it is essential that sufficient tolerance be present.

The next step in the preparation of the handle is to drill a $\frac{1}{8}$-inch hole to accommodate the brass brad. Together, the handle slot and brad hold the wheel in place, yet allow unimpaired movement. The action is similar to a horseman's spur.

Test the fit of the brad. If it is too loose, consider a slightly wider brad that will sink into the wood as it is tapped down. If the pointed end of the brad extends beyond the handle, a slight turning of the point with a pair of pliers (needle-nosed) will deflect the point back into the wood. A better axle is then the result.

Sanding of the handle is performed to remove rough surfaces and will impart a smooth surface pleasant to the touch.

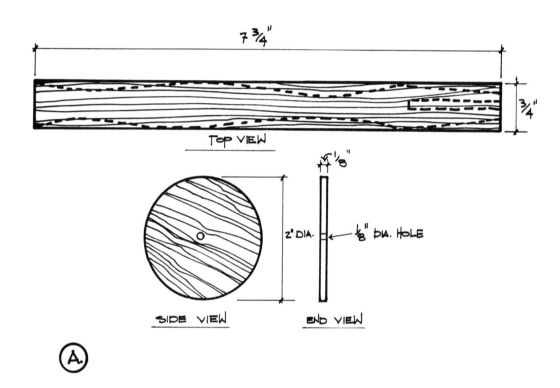

78

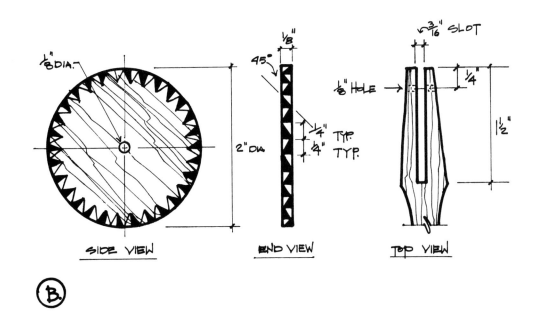

$\frac{1}{8}"$ DIA.

2" DIA

45°

$\frac{1}{8}"$

$\frac{1}{4}"$ TYP.

$\frac{1}{4}"$ TYP.

$\frac{3}{16}"$ SLOT

$\frac{1}{8}"$ HOLE

$\frac{1}{4}"$

$1\frac{1}{2}"$

SIDE VIEW

END VIEW

TOP VIEW

(B.)

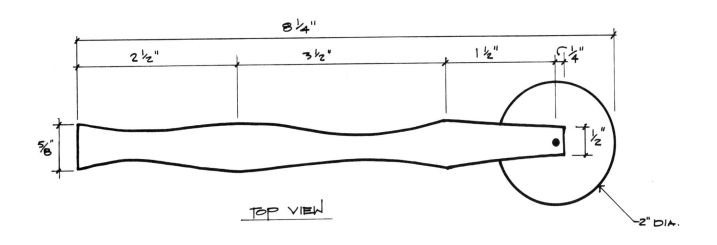

$8\frac{1}{4}"$

$2\frac{1}{2}"$

$3\frac{1}{2}"$

$1\frac{1}{2}"$

$\frac{1}{4}"$

$\frac{5}{8}"$

$\frac{1}{2}"$

TOP VIEW

2" DIA.

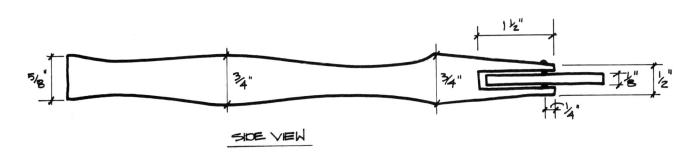

$1\frac{1}{2}"$

$\frac{5}{8}"$

$\frac{3}{4}"$

$\frac{3}{4}"$

$\frac{1}{8}"$

$\frac{1}{2}"$

$\frac{1}{4}"$

SIDE VIEW

(C)

SCANDINAVIAN BUTTER PADDLE

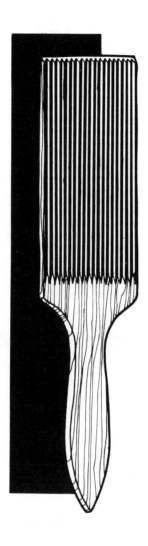

It is surprising how a small lump of cold butter can be quickly transformed into a decorative ball. A butter ball, is not only more decorative than a butter pat, but melts more slowly and preserves its shape, thereby providing a pleasing accent to any dish in which butter is a necessary ingredient. Very cold butter balls, fresh from the back of the refrigerator, can be placed in a thermal dish and left on the dining table for long periods; a thoughtful touch used by many inspired cooks. Two butter paddles are necessary to make each ball. The butter slice is placed on one of the grooved paddles. The other paddle is placed on top, and rotated in a clockwise movement, to slowly work the pat into a ball. The larger the butter pat, the larger the ball. A bit of deft practice and you can forget about ordinary swipes of butter for topping off waffles, Danish pastry, steamed broccoli, and airy French toast.

WOOD

The traditional wood for the butter paddle has been birch and justifiably so. Birch doesn't absorb grease. No birch available? Try oak, beech, maple, or even walnut, all of which can be worked with hand tools. **Raw wood should measure 2 inches wide by 9 inches in length. The thickness may vary from 3/16 to 3/8 inch.**

EQUIPMENT

Coping saw
C-clamp
Parting "V" tool to make ridges
Wood mallet
Sandpaper: grades 120, 220, 280, 400 (aluminum oxide paper)
Pencil #2
Ruler

PROCEDURE

On a piece of 3- by 10-inch paper, draw an outline of the butter paddle in accordance with Illustration A. Transfer the drawing from paper to wood. (See Chapter 3.) Secure the wood to the worktable with a C-clamp. If the stock is a true 2 inches wide, then allow the handle portion of the paddle to extend beyond the edge of the worktable by 5 inches. With the coping saw, cut away handle from surrounding wood to form what may look like a paintbrush handle. Loosen C-clamp and place the entire stock on the flat work surface and clamp in place. The clamp must not be positioned on the part that is to be cut with the parting tool. Two clamps may be required, if the wood is going to skate while being worked.

Approximately sixteen equal grooves are to be made with the parting tool. You will use the mallet to drive the tool along the wood in order to remove a fine paring of hardwood for each row. The grooves are V-shaped and are 1/8 inch deep. Keep your hand firmly planted on the parting tool, and apply light taps to the tip of the tool. Bring the parting tool up towards the end of the cut. The exit takes place with the last few taps and should be consistent for each row. All channels are 4½ inches in length. Although undesirable, the grooves may vary in depth, but do try to make cuts of uniform depth.

If you are a newcomer to carving with the parting tool, experiment on scraps for a while to develop a feeling for pressure, control, and maneuverability.

Sand the handle and the flat portion just above the grooves with graded sandpapers and finish off with the 400 aluminum oxide paper. No oiling or sealing is necessary.

As two paddles are required, simply repeat the above process, and, in about two hour's time, you will be rolling butter to everyone's delight, especially your own.

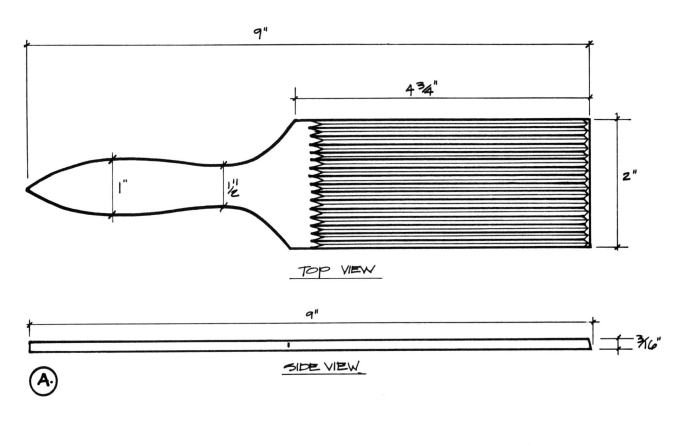

9"

4¾"

1"

1½"

2"

TOP VIEW

9"

3/16"

SIDE VIEW

Ⓐ.

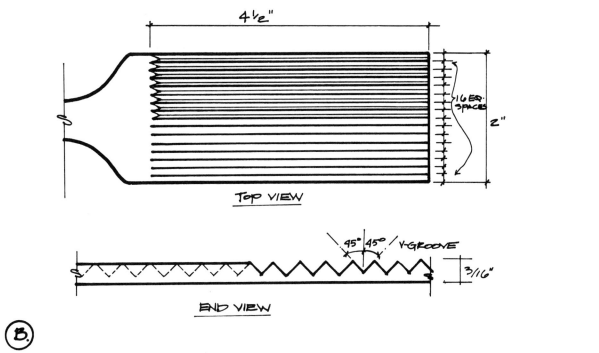

4½"

16 EQ.
SPACES

2"

TOP VIEW

95° 45° V-GROOVE

3/16"

END VIEW

Ⓑ.

MORTAR AND PESTLE

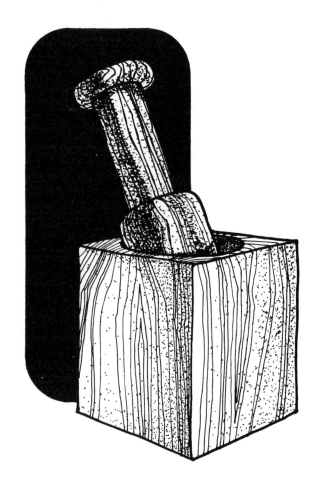

Just about every imaginable food can be enhanced with the delicate addition of herbs and spices. If you are fortunate enough to have a kitchen herb garden, pluck fresh herbs from the kitchen window ledge and gingerly grind them into tiny fragments by means of this mortar and pestle. Fennel, dill, sage, rosemary, cinnamon, parsley, spearmint, and a whole forest of edible herbs and spices can be prepared with this laminated mortar and pestle, made of assorted light and dark hardwoods, which have been oiled to take on a deep and lustrous exterior finish. Make herbal and spiced tea drinks, grind taragon to go with roast chicken, crush sweet marjoram for soups and stews, combine chervil and basil for egg and tomato dishes. With this utensil you can do it all and do it well.

WOOD

For the mortar, you will need to obtain two blocks of light- and dark-colored hardwood, measuring 3½ inches in height, 1¾ inches in width, and 3½ inches in depth. The pestle is made up of three pieces of light-colored hardwood. The top cap of the pestle measures 1½ inches in diameter and is round. The shank, also round, measures 1 inch in diameter and 3½ inches in length. The third piece of wood is the actual crusher part of the pestle and measures 1½ inches in diameter by 4 inches in length. All pieces should be purchased in their respective round form to obviate the need to shape by hand.

All three pieces of wood can conceivably be of dowel rods. The 1½-inch dowel is typical of the type used for closet coat hanger poles; it is likely to be found in home-supply stores. Wood-turned pieces, old fittings from discarded furniture, or scraps from a wood-turning company can provide you with dark hardwoods not obtainable in the majority of lumberyards. If, however, square or rectangular wood is your best alternative, then, by means of coarse wood files, you can bring the wood around to the above measurements. This is not all that difficult, but may be time-consuming. Each piece will need rotating by hand as filing is being done, and a caliper is used to gauge the diameter for accurate results.

EQUIPMENT

Coping saw or backsaw
C-clamp
Spoon-bit gouge
Wood mallet
Surform file or half-round wood rasp
Resorcinol wood glue
Small wood clamp for pressing wood together as it dries
Sandpaper: grades 120, 220, 280, 400 (aluminum oxide paper)
Vegetable oil (or mineral or olive oil)
Pencil #2
Ruler

PROCEDURE

The light- and dark-colored woods are placed flat on a table. Side by side, they are marked with a pencil to conform to the pattern and measurements given in Illustration A. The pencil line is the guideline by which you will make cuts with the spoon-bit gouge.

Clamp both stocks firmly to the work surface, and, with a mallet and gouge, begin to carve out the space. This space will serve as a well for the pestle, once the two blocks have been carved, sanded, and glued together. The important matter in carving the well is to remove only small chips after the general shape has been achieved. The radius at the bottom of the well must fit the contour of the pestle for a productive grinding action. Therefore, use the mallet with discretion, and tap lightly on the spoon-bit gouge. Once the interior hollow of both woods has been carved, begin to sand. Wrap 120 sandpaper around your forefinger and sand the concave portions of both blocks. Periodically, bring both blocks together, so that they interface and form a round and smooth well. Keep both faces absolutely flat, as the two surfaces will be glued to make a cubical mortar. Rough spots or high areas are best dealt with by means of the coarse sandpaper. Sand with the finer papers, grades 220 through the fine 400 aluminum oxide paper. You may include the outside of the blocks as well in this operation.

Apply a small amount of resorcinol glue (the generic name) to both surfaces that are to be assembled. Application of the glue is best done by spreading the glue with something flat, such as a wooden ice cream pop stick. A thin veneer of glue is all that is required, but it must be spread over the entire face of both blocks. Press both blocks together, clamp with the wood clamp, and let stand for twenty-four hours.

The pestle is made by gluing three unrelated sizes of round wood together to form one tool, which will resemble a plunger. This is done in the following manner: lay out the three pieces of wood on the worktable. (Check measurements before assembly). Clamp the 4-inch dowel first by means of a C-clamp or table vise. Use a 1-inch drill

bit or drill bit attachment to bore a 1-inch-deep hole in the top end of the rod. This hole is to receive the shank. The tip of the large dowel is shaped to form a blunt tip similar to the nose of a large bullet. The Surform file or a half-round wood rasp will do the job quite well. Continue to check the fit by inserting the worked tip of the pestle into the well of the mortar. Fine adjustments will undoubtedly need to be made.

Cut the shank to appropriate size as depicted. Apply a thin veneer of resorcinol glue to the drilled end of the pestle and install the shank, which has previously been cut to proper length. Allow to stand. No clamping should be necessary if the fit is firm. Of course, if the fit is less than ideal (a bit of play exists), then clamp the wood with the same wood clamp. Drying time is twenty-four hours. The cap of the pestle, which rests in the user's palm, may be glued on the shank while the procedure for fitting the shank in the pestle is done to make the operation happen at one time. Illustration D shows the assembly, which is a whole lot easier to do than it is to describe. Ease the edge of the cap with 120 sandpaper, and then, with 220, sand the

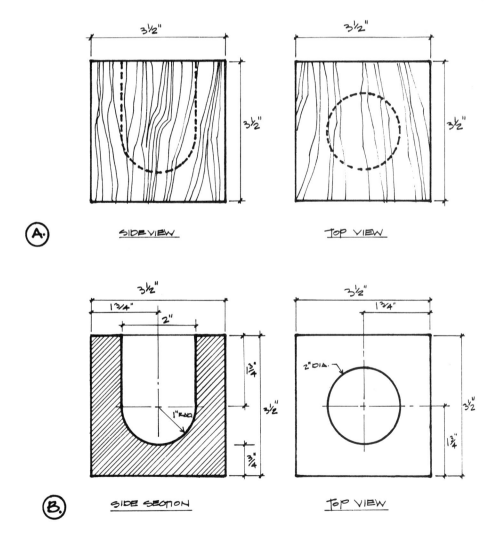

83

entire pestle. Finish the sanding steps with 280 and 400 sandpaper.

The aperture of the mortar is twice the diameter of the pestle's tip. This allows for a rolling/grinding motion, which is the heart of the utensil.

The mortar should be cleaned with a dry, stiff bristle brush before and after each use. Mint tea with traces of dill weed makes for an odd taste, but can be altogether avoided by an occasional dry scour.

The exterior of the mortar should have a small amount of vegetable oil rubbed into its surface to preserve the wood. Do not wash the mortar or pestle in water, as the wood will likely expand and might possibly develop small cracks. The resorcinol glue, although waterproof, is a brittle type, and wood expansion is likely to break the bond. By following this precaution, your mortar and pestle will last for an indefinite number of years and will age gracefully.

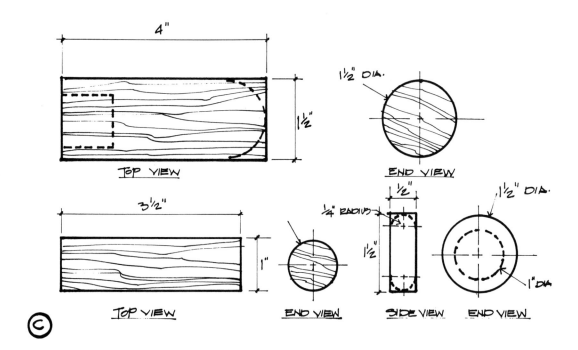

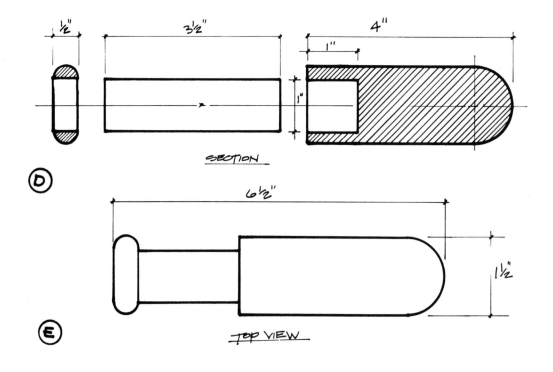

JUICE EXTRACTOR AND MASHER

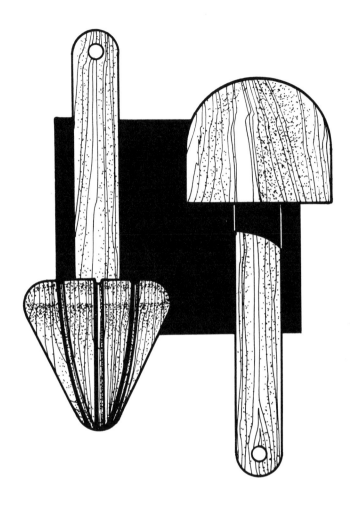

Juice extractors are relatively specialized implements. They are the perfect tool for releasing vitamin-rich juices from citrus fruits, such as oranges, lemons, grapefruits, and tangerines, but they won't make a dent in a carrot and will completely annihilate grapes. Juice directly from the fruit can hardly be fresher, nor could it taste better.

Illustrated are two versions of the juice extractor. The version with the thin, fluted sides is used with citrus fruits. It enables the juices to flow downwards through the channels into a receptacle. The beefier version is used more for mashing fruits and vegetables, such as tomatoes, strawberries, apples, raspberries, cherries, and cranberries. Both utensils are well suited to their function, which is to reduce foods so as to extract their essences for beverages and as flavoring for other foods.

WOOD

Juices from most of the above fruits and vegetables will stain practically any wood you can think of, unless it has been sealed with a synthetic varnish or wood sealer. Sealing is to be discouraged, however, because of the toxic properties in sealers, stains, varnishes, shellac, and the like. Therefore, any good hardwood will fit the bill, and oak is a particularly beautiful wood, discolorations and all. The heads from both juice extractors come from identically sized cubes. **The raw wood measures 3 inches wide by 3 inches deep by 2½ inches high. Handles are to be 6½ inches in length and 1 inch in diameter.**

EQUIPMENT

Coping saw
C-Clamp or table vise
¼-inch and 1-inch drill bit and hand or power drill
Surform wood file or half-round wood rasp
Scribing gouge and mallet (for extractor only)
Sandpaper: grades 120, 220, 280, 400 (aluminum oxide paper)
Waterproof white glue
Pencil #2
Ruler

PROCEDURE

The following description is based on the masher/extractor. The fluted version varies only in the treatment for the head. Directions for the masher are given first, followed by directions for the extractor.

On paper, first measure and draw the pattern. Copy the measurements on the wood stock. With the block for the head clamped to the work surface, locate the center of the top face. With a 1-inch drill bit or drill bit attachment, bore a hole to a depth of 1 inch. The handle will be inserted in this hole, which eventually will be partially covered with waterproof glue.

Clamp the block to a worktable, and, with the wood file, begin to shape the head, so that it takes on a round configuration. After several passes with the file, rotate the stock to ensure uniform circumference. Continue to file until the entire surface resembles Illustration A, both side and end views. Sanding with grade 120 paper will make a considerably smoother surface and will eliminate unwanted highspots, which will be likely to trap juices. The finished results will loosely resemble a mushroom head with parallel sides.

The 1-inch-diameter handle is cut to the prescribed length, lightly sanded, and inserted into the hole of the extractor head immediately after a small amount (½ ounce) of glue is rubbed inside the hole, so that all surfaces are covered. If the handle resists your efforts as it is being fitted, then lightly tap the opposite end with a wood mallet to make the assembly a snug and correct one. If you wish, a hole may be drilled in the handle's end for hanging. This is best done before head and handle are assembled, since the wood is more easily handled at that stage.

Sand the entire tool with 220, 280, and 400 sandpaper. The smoother the finish, the less the open grain will be likely to absorb juices beyond control. Refer to the section on finishes in Chapter 3 for information on how to bleach

wood the natural way, if the discoloration gets to you and you would like to have a lighter appearance.

The juice extractor, in principle, is made in the same manner as the juice masher. The shape is slightly different, and the channeled sides are unique to the tool's function. The block of wood is identical in size to the masher. However, the taper of the head is more radical. With the Surform file, shape the head so that it resembles the one featured in the illustration. When you consider what the

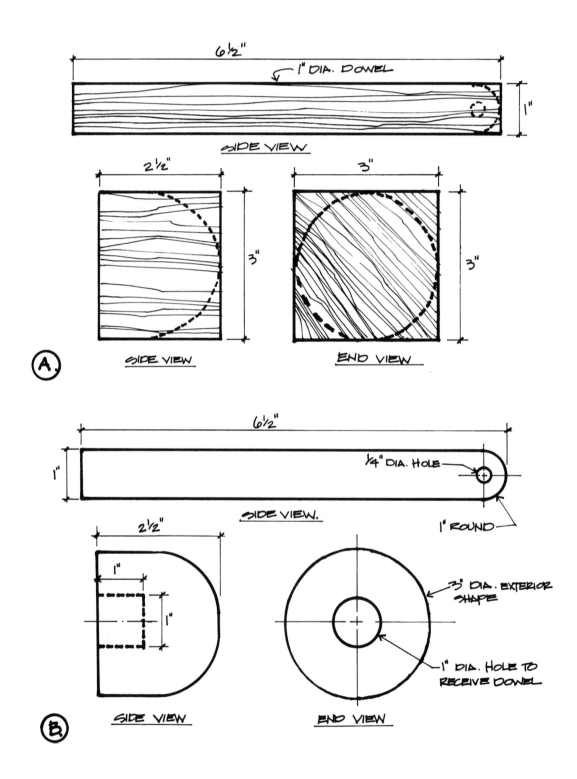

tool must do, the shape of the head is obvious; it must bore its way into the heart of the citrus fruit. The utensil is then turned, creating a shredding action, which frees the juice from the fruit's fibrous cells. The bottom edge of the head is radiused in order for the juice to run inwards, thereby concentrating the flow within a very narrow space.

The channels, or grooves, are best made with a scribing gouge, which is designed to make thin channels in wood.

The hardness of the wood will necessitate the use of a mallet in order to work the chisel with some degree of control. The head is clamped to prevent the stock from rolling. Ideally, the channels are equidistant from one another, but this is not critical to the tool's function.

Sand the finished product after assembly, as you would for the masher.

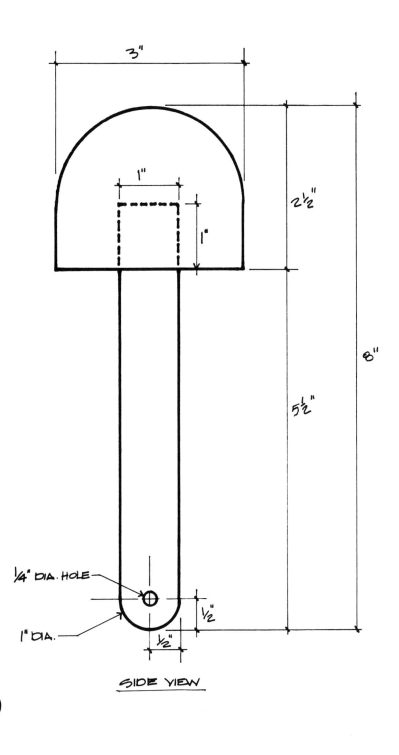

SIDE VIEW

Ⓒ

JAPANESE MALLET

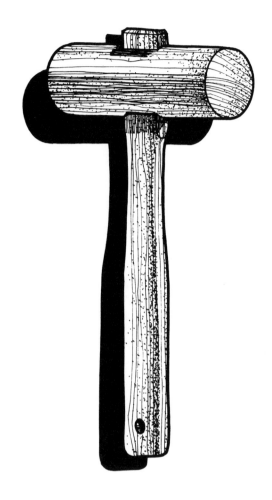

Fresh-water fish tend to be more tender than many ocean fish, and the latter occasionally need an assist from the chef in order to render the meat more supple and flaky. Turbot, flounder, rock cod, and salmon all benefit from a few slams with the Japanese mallet. Even the most resilient fish, placed between a couple of sheets of durable waxed paper and given a few glancing blows distributed over its entire flesh, will be more edible.

The Japanese mallet can be used to flatten a split chicken just prior to broiling or to drive a stubborn cork back into a wine bottle. As an ice crusher, this hickory version takes no back seat. It can be quite an assertive device when it comes time to reduce ice cubes to crushed ice for the home ice cream maker.

WOOD
The handle for the mallet is made of hickory or maple; both woods are noted for their density and give a hefty feel

when in hand. **The wood should measure 12 inches in length, ⅞ inch in width, and ½ inch in height. The head is composed of the same wood, measuring 1¼ inches in diameter and 4¼ inches in overall length.**

EQUIPMENT
Coping saw
C-clamp or table vise
Surform flat wood file
Small ½-inch flat wood file
¼-inch and ⅞-inch drill bit or drill bit attachment and hand
  or power drill
Sandpaper: grades 120, 220, 280, 400 (aluminum oxide
  paper)
Pencil #2
Ruler

PROCEDURE
The handle for the mallet is rectangular in shape, rather than round like a traditional wood mallet. The angle of the handle is thus kept in proper orientation to the mallet head. With the coping saw, cut the handle to the exact measurements given in Illustration A, top and side view. Three inches of one end of the handle are then filed with the Surform file to gently taper towards the tip, which must be no less than ⅞ inch in height. Diagram B, top view, depicts the shape and pinpoints the spot where the ¼-inch hole is to be drilled, which enables the utensil to be hung from a nail or peg or as part of a utensil display.

The mallet head is cylindrical in shape and can be shaped from square stock by means of the Surform file. Remember to frequently rotate the stock in order to arrive at a true round rod. The tips of the mallet are beveled to keep the edge of the wood from fraying as the result of blows missing their intended mark and glancing off a harder surface.

The trick here is to make a square hole, which is no trick at all, provided you follow these simple steps: clamp the round head to the work surface, so that no movement is possible. With a pencil and ruler, draw a square measuring ⅞ inch wide and ½ inch high. With a ½-inch drill bit, bore two holes in the wood, one to the left of the square and one to the right. Both holes should overlap one another in order to stay within the ⅞-inch limitation. What results is a rectangular hole with four radiused corners. By means of a ½-inch flat wood file, slowly work the file back and forth in the hole to remove the radius and to leave in its place four corners with true right angles—a true rectangle. The hole is now as true as the head of the mallet's handle and should fit neatly over the top. In order to eliminate the need for a peg to keep the handle in place, it will be necessary to force the head down on the stem of the handle. A wood-carving or rubber-head mallet should be used to apply alternating taps on the right and left sides of the head gently driving the movement downwards.

Hickory and maple, like so many other woods, swell when saturated with water. Therefore, to lock the woods together, allow the top end, fitted with the head, to sit for a couple of hours in a tub or warm water. Remove and let dry near a warm spot of the workshop in direct sunlight. The expansion of the wood will create a firm bond, and no further effort is required. As the illustration depicts, the handle protrudes beyond the top plane of the hammer. It is to be left this way. Japanese joinery is an art that sidesteps the need for nails and other fastening hardware. The beauty of the design is part of the tool's integrity and is to be appreciated for its open, honest attention to detail.

Sand all surfaces, starting with grade 120 and then working into the finer grades, finishing up with 400. No oiling or sealing of any kind is required.

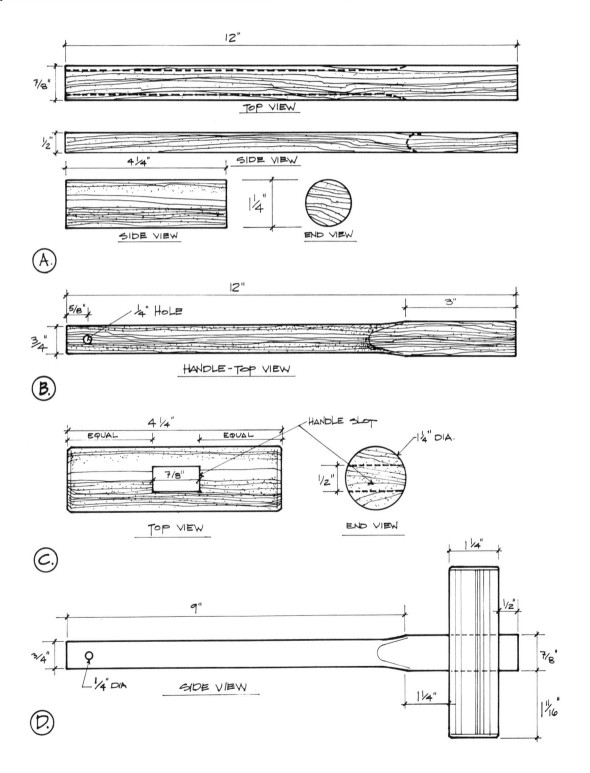

SPICE SIEVE

American Colonists, Shakers, and newly arrived immigrants used sieves in practically all modes of food preparation. Tiny sieves for medicine powders were staple items for the rural physician. Made of horsehair long before the time when metal strands were introduced, sieves sifted such sundry items as sugar, salt, herbs, spices, soda, and meals. Grandma in the kitchen and Grandpa in the barn both had their sieves. Sieving involves texture changes and is by no means reserved for dry goods. Vegetable and fruit purees are also sieved and can provide a finer gradation of texture. Often, sieves and strainers are used interchangeably, though, by definition, the strainer is designed to separate liquids from solids. No discerning cook can get by without a sieve as it is indispensable in the making of practically all flour and bakery products, from rolls, croissants, pie dough, and fresh breads, to the most delicate of French pastries.

Two considerations must be weighed before you build your own sieve. Firstly, the mesh you choose should be fine enough to prevent unwanted ingredients, such as seeds, stems, and skins, from passing through. Secondly, the sieve must be in proportion to the bowl, kettle, dish, or pan over which it is to be used. Ideally, several sieves with mesh ranging from fine to coarse should be made in various sized frames to fit any occasion.

WOOD AND OTHER MATERIALS

In its simplest form, the sieve is a rectangular frame with screen mesh taughtly stretched over the top. On the upper surface of the frame, another frame is attached to conceal the rough ends of the screen. **The wood for the lower frame consists of four pieces: two 10½- by 2½- by 1-inch pieces of hardwood and two 6½- by 2½- by 1-inch pieces of identical wood. The top frame consists of the following: two 10½- by ¾- by 1-inch pieces of hardwood and two 6½- by ¾- by 1-inch strips of the same wood of your choice. The screen should be brass or stainless steel and twenty to thirty-five strands of wire per inch makes the most useful mesh. A piece 5½ by 9½ inches is needed.**

EQUIPMENT

Backsaw
Coping saw
Claw hammer
Screwdriver
Wood clamps, 2
Staple gun ³⁄₁₆-inch to ¼-inch brass staples (nontarnishing)
Waterproof wood glue or animal hide glue
¼-inch drill bit and hand or power drill
Woodscrews, flathead type, ⅜ inch
Pencil #2
Ruler
Miter Box

PROCEDURE

Pre-measure and cut all parts to fit the prescribed lengths. With the backsaw, miter all wood strips (ends) to 45-degree angles. In order to have an exact fit (to form a rectangle) a miter box may be used.

The bottom frame is laid out on the worktable in its respective position of assembly. With the coping saw, proceed to cut the inner curve of the bottom of each wood strip to form the legs of the sieve. Illustration A gives the radius and inner dimension for the frame. Simply follow the measurements. The ½-inch radius is not critical, but gives a pleasing shape to the leg. The frame is assembled by means of light glue application to the ends of the strips, which are then assembled and clamped with the two wood clamps on extreme edges of the frame. After the frame glue has completely dried, the clamps are removed.

Apply the screen mesh with the help of the staple gun and staples. Follow the pattern shown in Illustration C.

The top frame is measured, cut, and glued in the above manner. It too must be clamped and allowed sufficient drying time. When dry, the frame is placed on top of the frame and four ¼-inch holes are drilled to accept the wood screws. The heads of the screws are to be flush with the surface of the wood or they can be countersunk by means of a larger drill bit used to bore a slightly wider hole to accommodate the screw's head.

The wood strips are easily sanded before assembly, but, because of the simple configuration of the sieve, it may be sanded after it is built. Sealing with vegetable oil will close some of the wood's pores.

To remove a damaged screen, unscrew the four wood screws, lift the top off of the frame, and install a new piece. Replace the top frame in the same manner as was done in the initial installation. Of course, your measurements may be changed depending on how you intend to use the sieve, but the procedure remains the same.

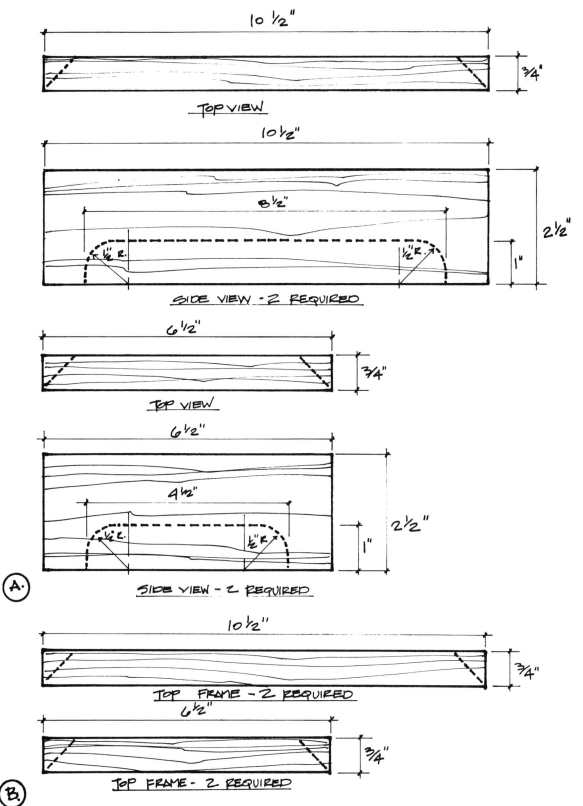

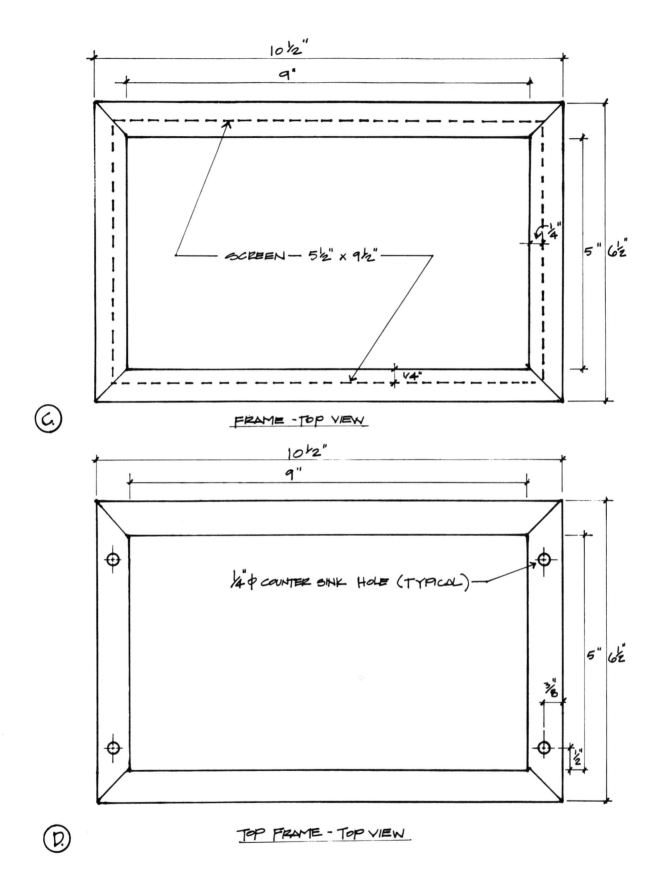

10½"

9"

5" 6½"

¼"

¼"

SCREEN — 5½" x 9½"

C. FRAME - TOP VIEW

10½"

9"

5" 6½"

¼" ⌀ COUNTER SINK HOLE (TYPICAL)

⅜"

½"

D. TOP FRAME - TOP VIEW

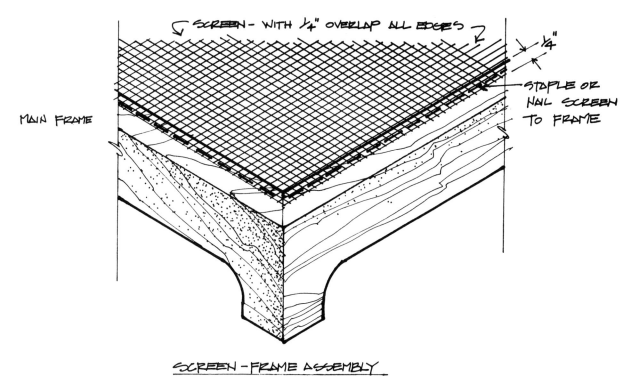

SCREEN — WITH ¼" OVERLAP ALL EDGES

¼"

STAPLE OR
NAIL SCREEN
TO FRAME

MAIN FRAME

SCREEN — FRAME ASSEMBLY

E.

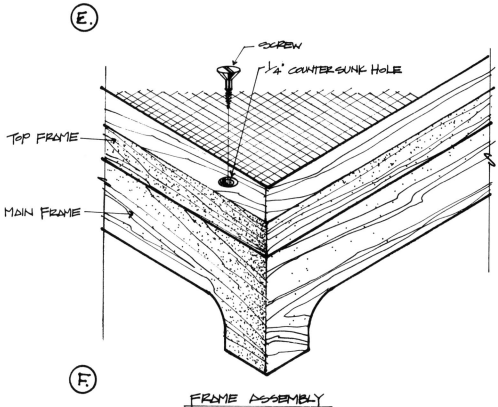

SCREW

¼" COUNTERSUNK HOLE

TOP FRAME

MAIN FRAME

F.

FRAME ASSEMBLY

93

KIBBI HAMMER

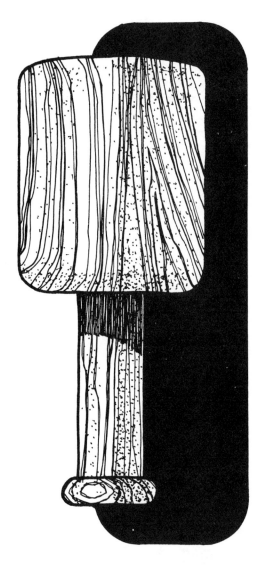

also round, measures 4¼ inches in diameter and is 5 inches long. The tip of the handle is neatly capped off with a round, button-shaped oak fitting measuring 2 inches in diameter and ¾ inch in thickness.

EQUIPMENT

Coping saw
Large wood clamp or table vise
Compass fitted with pencil lead
1½-inch-diameter drill bit accessory and hand or power drill
Flat wood file
Animal hide glue
Wood mallet
Sandpaper: grades 120, 220, 280, 400 (aluminum oxide paper)
Vegetable oil (or mineral or olive oil)
Soft, lint-free cloth
Pencil #2
Ruler

PROCEDURE

The cubical head, which initially is a block of wood, is cut by means of the coping saw. The wood is positioned with the top of the hammer head facing up and is clamped in place with the wood clamp. The compass is divided to create a 4¼-inch-diameter circle and is drawn as such on the top surface. Loosen the stock, and move the wood to its side; clamp once again. Cut out a cylindrical shape by rotating the stock every 90 degrees. Of course, if you have access to a bandsaw fitted with a wood-cutting blade, the whole operation goes much smoother and faster. With one flat side facing upwards, drill a 1½-inch hole in the center of the head to a depth of 2 inches.

The handle (6 by 1½ inches in diameter) is inserted or knocked in place with the mallet into the preglued and predrilled hole and is allowed to stand for twenty-four hours. If glue oozes from the join, simply wipe away the residual smear with a damp cloth; this must be done quickly, before the hide glue sets up, or it will stain the tool's handle or underside.

The 2-inch-wide cap is now drilled with the same drill bit attachment to a depth of ⅜ inch. Cover the inside of the fresh hole with hide glue, insert over handle's exposed end, and let stand overnight.

All surfaces are thoroughly filed and sanded. With a hammer of this bulk and build, you want to be assured that it feels one hundred percent smooth in your hand. A small amount of vegetable oil is applied with a soft cloth and worked for twenty minutes into the wood's pores. One application is enough—too much oil and the tool is likely to leave your hand during a precious blow and create its own path for movement.

For those occasions when, short of jumping up and down on the all-too-coarse meat, you don't know what to do, consider the kibbi hammer. While the usual mallets are fine for flattening and thinning out cube steak or chicken, on occasion, a stouter bludgeon comes in handy.

In a book on the foods of Lebanon, I came across a pounder used in the preparation of lamb, the principal food in the dish called *kibbi*, Lebanon's national dish. In kibbi, the meat is often eaten raw, pounded together with bulgur wheat. In honor of this famous dish I have named this mallet a "kibbi hammer."

WOOD

Both handle and mallet head are made of ash or oak. Traditionally, hardwood is used for such a tool. The handle is **round, 1½ inches in diameter, and 6 inches in length.** The short handle makes the tool easier to wield. **The head,**

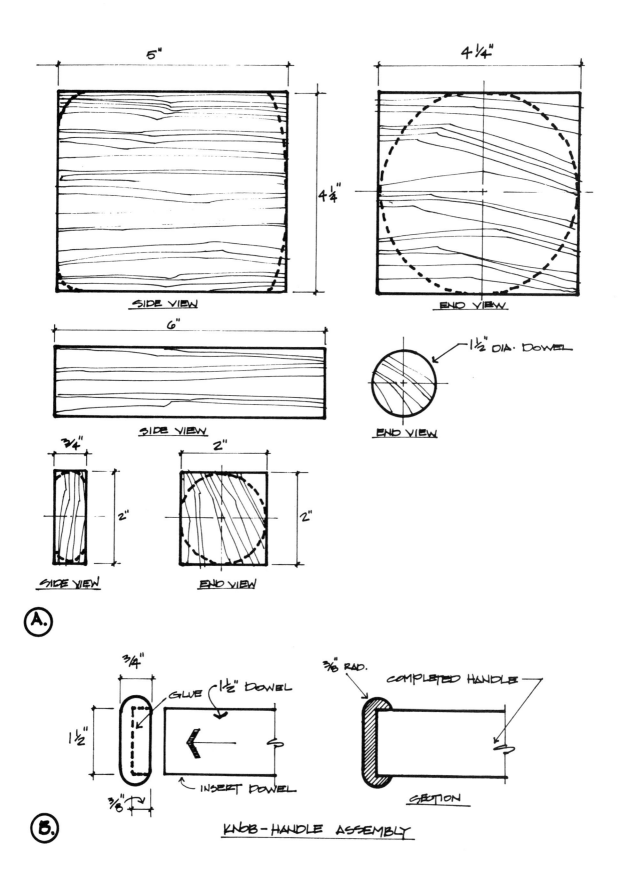

5"

4¼"

SIDE VIEW

4¼"

4¼"

END VIEW

6"

SIDE VIEW

1½" DIA. DOWEL

END VIEW

¾"

2"

2"

2"

2"

SIDE VIEW

END VIEW

A.

¾"

GLUE 1½" DOWEL

1½"

⅜"

INSERT DOWEL

⅜" RAD.

COMPLETED HANDLE

SECTION

B.

KNOB-HANDLE ASSEMBLY

95

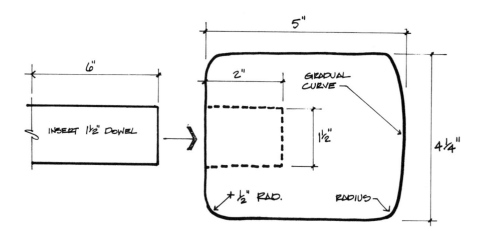

5"

2"

GRADUAL
CURVE

INSERT 1½" DOWEL

6"

1½"

4¼"

½" RAD.

RADIUS

MALLET HEAD - HANDLE ASSEMBLY.

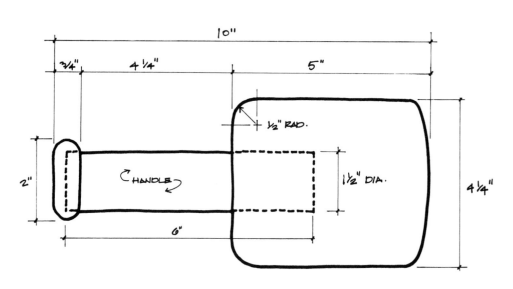

10"

¾"

4¼"

5"

½" RAD.

HANDLE

1½" DIA.

4¼"

2"

6"

TOP VIEW

BUTCHER BLOCK/ SERVING TRAY

This tray was designed not only to serve up food, but also to be of assistance in its preparation. Handles are designed right into the tray which also has a depressed area to prevent juices, crumbs, sauces, and glasses from sliding off. It is handsome enough to be left on the dining table until it's time to clear the dishes, at which point it serves as a bussing tray as well. It has a stout and hefty appearance and will last for years, improving with use and age. The surface should be washed with a damp rag and a small amount of detergent to keep food from being too deeply absorbed.

WOOD

Hardwoods are indicated for this project because they will resist scratches and in an all-around way will last longer. The illustration depicts a ribbon effect which is achieved by combining oak and walnut in alternating laminations. The number of pieces used for the lamination is at the discretion of the woodworker. The one shown here was made with twelve, while Illustration A depicts a board made with ten laminated pieces.

If ten strips of wood are to be used, each will measure 18 inches plus by alternating strips of equal length but measuring ¾ inch and 1½ inch in width. The height of each strip is 1½ inches. Allow for a slightly smaller overall dimension due to sanding. This explains the plus dimension given in the length measurement.

EQUIPMENT

Handsaw
Woodworker's waterproof glue
2 wood clamps
Mallet
Round wood gouge
Electric hand drill with 1-inch bit or bit attachment
Flatwood file
Keyhole saw
Surform wood file
Sandpaper: grades 80, 120, 220
Carborundum paper: grades 400 and 600
Pencil #2
Ruler

PROCEDURE

Dimension, mark and saw all pieces of wood to conform to required sizes, as depicted in Illustration A. Apply glue to all sides to be laminated and clamp with the two wood clamps tightly secured. Remove all residual glue oozing from joins with a damp and lint-free rag. Allow to stand in room temperature until thoroughly dry, about twenty-four hours.

With the mallet and wood gouge proceed to carve out the middle area to a depth of ½ inch, as indicated in Diagram B. Note the radius of the corners. The rounded corners greatly facilitate cleaning. Therefore, care should be taken to make these as true and smooth as is possible.

Next, drill two holes opposite one another for each handle. Remove the wood separating the two holes by repeatedly drilling or by means of a keyhole saw. File smooth with the flat wood file. Repeat this step for the other handle.

Corners of the tray are rounded with the Surform wood file. Spend some time sanding all surfaces of the tray, beginning with the coarser grade of sandpaper. Then graduate to the finer grades and finish with carborundum paper grades 400 and 600 respectively.

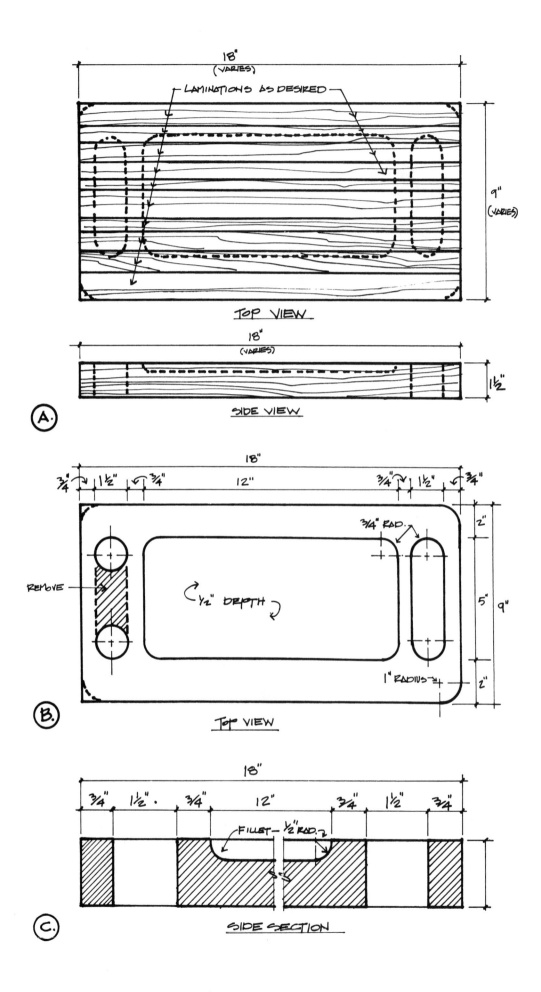

18"
(VARIES)

LAMINATIONS AS DESIRED

9"
(VARIES)

TOP VIEW

18"
(VARIES)

1½"

SIDE VIEW

(A.)

18"

¾"   1½"   ¾"   12"   ¾"   1½"   ¾"

¾" RAD.

2"

REMOVE

½" DEPTH

5"   9"

1" RADIUS

2"

(B.)   TOP VIEW

18"

¾"   1½"   ¾"   12"   ¾"   1½"   ¾"

FILLET — ½" RAD.

(C.)   SIDE SECTION

7.
Accessories for Storage and Display

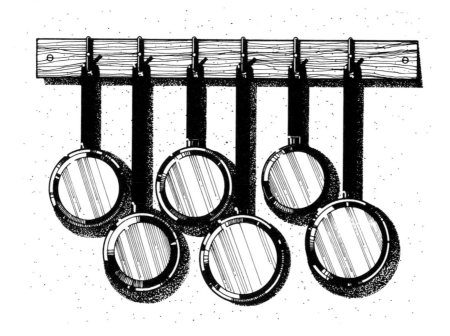

SPICE BOTTLE

A friend who is a great authority on food once told me that he never fails to be surprised when he encounters other cooks who insist on storing fine spices in plastic or cardboard containers. Nothing of the original fragrance and aroma remains for very long. These containers have little appeal beyond the fact that they were disposable once used. We discussed the merits of wood and its ability to retain the essential fragrances and odors of spices and herbs because of the wood's porosity. Since that time, I have always tried to use wood bottles for this purpose.

The simplest wood bottle one can make with a round shape is given here. It is an excellent sealer and reveals the virtue of simple shapes and objects.

WOOD AND OTHER MATERIALS

Select birch, ash, beech, or oak. Softwood, such as pine or Douglas fir, is also useful because it is easier to work from the craftsman's viewpoint. **A block of wood measuring 3 inches long by 2 inches high by 2 inches deep** is needed before the shaping process begins. **A round cork with a diameter of 1¼ inches is used as the sealer.** The small ball used to cap the bottle is nothing more than a cork ball which can easily be stuffed into the bottle's opening.

EQUIPMENT

Coping saw
C-clamp or table vise
1½-inch drill bit or drill bit accessory and hand or power drill
Flat wood file
Sandpaper: grades 120, 220, 280, 400 (aluminum oxide paper)
Pencil #2
Ruler

PROCEDURE

Use a ruler and pencil to locate the center of the block, which is to be locked in a vise or clamp in an upright position. Mark the center. With the drill and bit, bore a 1½-inch-wide hole to a depth of 2 inches. Wrap a piece of masking tape around the drill bit at the 2-inch mark in order to accurately gauge the correct measurement. Remove the stock from the vise and clamp so that sawing with the coping saw can be carried out by carefully rotating the block every 45 degrees. The objective is to cut a round cylinder from the square block to give the bottle its finished shape. Illustrations A and B reveal the final form.

If the round shape is a bit uneven, use the wood file to smoothen out high surfaces of the block. Filing is to be done lightly.

Once a round cylinder has been made, begin to sand with the coarse sandpaper and work up to the finer grades. Finish off with grade 400 aluminum oxide paper. The inside of the bottle should not need any additional sanding. Check cork for fit.

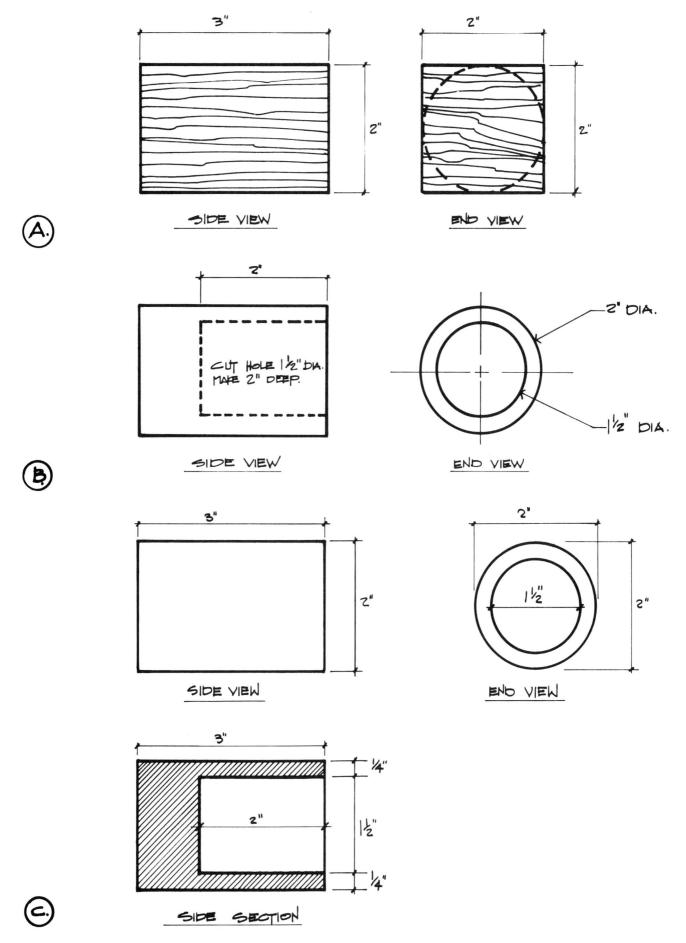

A.

SIDE VIEW   END VIEW

3"   2"

2"   2"

B.

SIDE VIEW   END VIEW

2"

CUT HOLE 1½" DIA.
MAKE 2" DEEP.

2" DIA.

1½" DIA.

C.

SIDE VIEW   END VIEW

3"   2"

2"   1½"   2"

SIDE SECTION

3"

¼"

2"

1½"

¼"

SMALL SPICE JAR

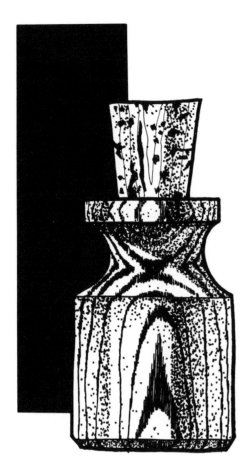

Spice jars seem to be more numerous than any of the other boxes likely to be found in the kitchen pantry. The first natural inclination is to open a spice box and smell the fragrance of the old spice, either the spice itself or the powder that still clings to the wood. An array of spice bottles can dress up a kitchen and, at the same time, put before the cook a rather tempting display of choices. The spice jar pictured here is quite small and is to be used for concentrated powders, such as saffron, paprika, and the like.

Review the spice bottle in the preceding project to acquaint yourself with the working procedure required to make small round bottles without the aid of a wood lathe (a machine usually not found in the wood hobbyists trove of hand and power equipment). The objective is to be able

to make the utensil without elaborate machinery and by means of simple handtools.

With this spice bottle the major differences lie in the indented ring on the upper portion of the jar and the overall inner diameter of the bottle. A cork of a different shape is used, but in principle it is identical to the example just described.

WOOD
Maple is a good common wood to consider when making the smaller spice jar. Some jars, however, can be made of birch, ash, beech, or a more ornamental version can be made of bird's eye maple. You will need a **2⅛- by 2¾-inch piece of wood.**

EQUIPMENT
Coping saw
C-clamp or table vise
⅞-inch drill bit or drill bit accessory and hand or power drill
Flat wood file
Rattail wood file
Sandpaper: grades 120, 220, 280, 400 (aluminum oxide paper)
Steel wool: grade 00
Pencil #2
Ruler

PROCEDURE
Review the procedure in the preceding example to obtain the basic shape. In place of the 1½-inch-diameter hole substitute a ⅞-inch drill bit and bore a hole in the center of the block to a depth of 2¼ inches. The bottom of the hole will have a slight depression owing to the pointed tip of the drill bit.

The radius along the upper portion of the wood jar is achieved with a rattail file of medium coarseness. The file is moved backwards and forwards a number of times. After a noticeable dent has been made, rotate the cylinder of wood and continue to file until the same depth is obtained. Remove the jar and continue to lightly file the ring with the jar in one hand, the file in the other.

Ease the bottom of the jar to a 45-degree angle. The surface area affected measures ⅛ inch.

File rough areas first. Sand the entire bottle with 120 sandpaper and continue to sand with the finer papers. The inside of the bottle should not only be sanded with fine sandpaper (280, 400), but should also have a smooth finish achieved by the use of grade 00 steel wool.

No sealing or additional finishing is required.

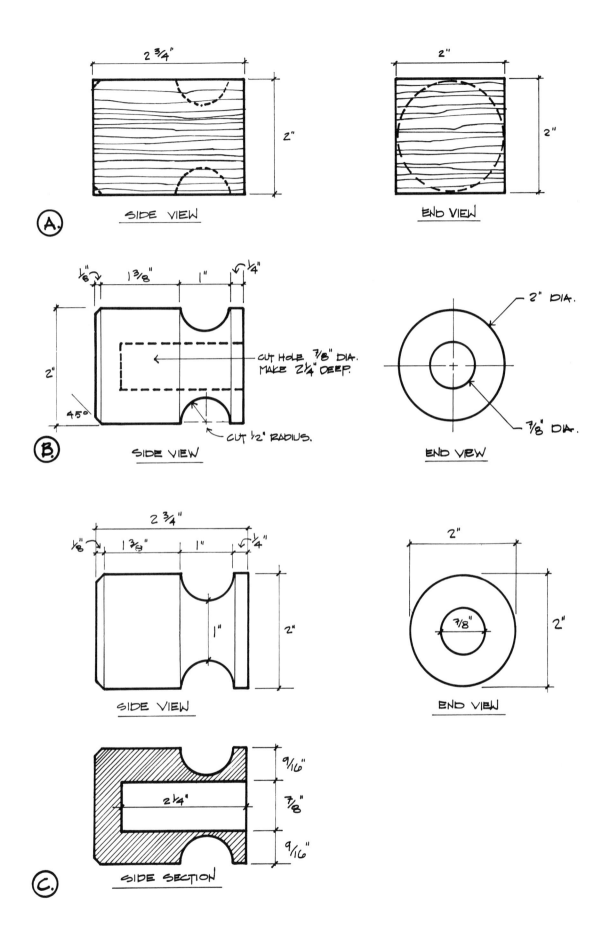

A.

2 3/4"

2"

2"

SIDE VIEW

2"

2"

END VIEW

B.

1/8" 1 3/8" 1" 1/4"

2"

45°

CUT HOLE 7/8" DIA.
MAKE 2 1/4" DEEP.

CUT 1/2" RADIUS.

SIDE VIEW

2" DIA.

7/8" DIA.

END VIEW

C.

2 3/4"

1/8" 1 3/8" 1" 1/4"

1"

2"

SIDE VIEW

2"

7/8"

2"

END VIEW

9/16"

2 1/4"

7/8"

9/16"

SIDE SECTION

WALL-MOUNTED
PAN RACK

Why hang pictures on the wall when you could hang a good-looking collection of pans? Arrange the pans according to frequency of use and size on this easily made rack. The rack is simply one strip of oak, easily installed with two bolts. The pan hooks can be slid to the right or left to make room for a variety of sizes.

WOOD AND OTHER MATERIALS

You will need one piece of solid oak measuring **22 by 2 by ⅜ inches.** Commercial pan hooks or the equivalent are used to hold the handles on the rack. The bracket can be mounted to the kitchen wall with long wood screws or molly bolts equipped with spreading flanges for greater strength.

EQUIPMENT

Backsaw
Handsaw, 24 to 26 inches in length
Ruler
Hammer
Vise (table mounted)
¼-inch drill bit and hand or power drill
Sandpaper: grades 120, 220, 280, 400 (aluminum oxide paper)
Pencil #2
Tape measure

PROCEDURE

Measure, mark, and cut the oak to the required size. Ease the top-front edge only with grade 120 sandpaper. It is over this edge that the hooks will hang. Hooks will be bent to conform to the shape of the edge and this is to be done last. See Illustration B.

Using the handsaw, cut a ⅛-inch-wide groove along the top surface of the oak bracket to a depth of ½ inch. Most handsaws have a blade that measures $^1/_{16}$ inch in thickness. Therefore, two small grooves will need to be cut in order to make one large groove to meet the specified ⅛ inch width.

Following the measurements given in Illustration B, front view, drill two holes with a 1¼-inch-diameter drill bit.

Rods for the hooks can be cut from industrial-strength copper or brass or cold-rolled steel, which is much harder, or you can use commercial hooks. The rods are stocked by the larger hardware stores in most cities. Rods are bent in a vise with pliers or hammered into an S shape.

Finishing the oak is optional. A finish is likely to be scratched after several months of continuous use, thereby necessitating an occasional resurfacing. The oak may be left in its natural unfinished state, if desired.

Mount the finished unit on the kitchen wall with 2½-inch flathead ¼-inch wood screws. If your unit is going to be used to hold very heavy pots and pans, then install using traditional Molly bolts. Hardware stores stock them. You will need to locate wall studs for best placement. Studs are usually spaced 16 inches apart from one another.

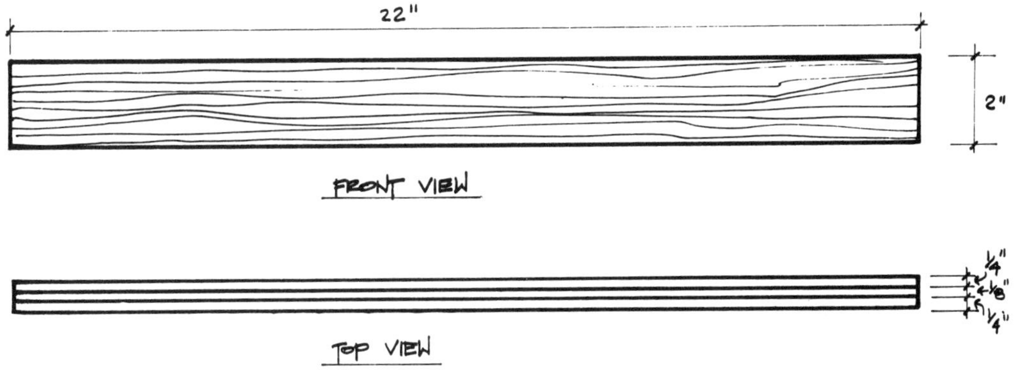
22"
2"
FRONT VIEW
1/4"
1/8"
1/4"
TOP VIEW

A.

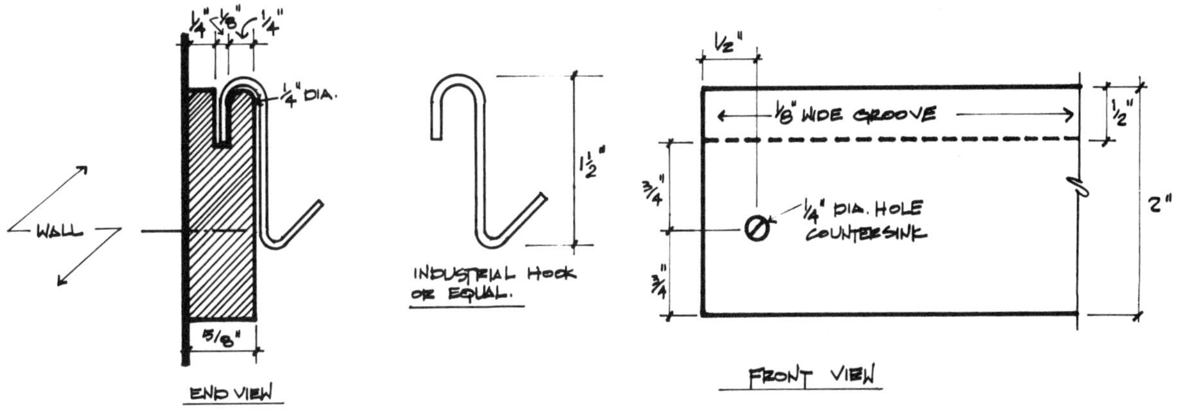
1/4"
1/8"
1/4"
1/4" DIA.
WALL
5/8"
END VIEW
1 1/2"
INDUSTRIAL HOOK OR EQUAL.
1/2"
1/8" WIDE GROOVE
1/2"
3/4"
1/4" DIA. HOLE COUNTERSINK
3/4"
2"
FRONT VIEW

B.

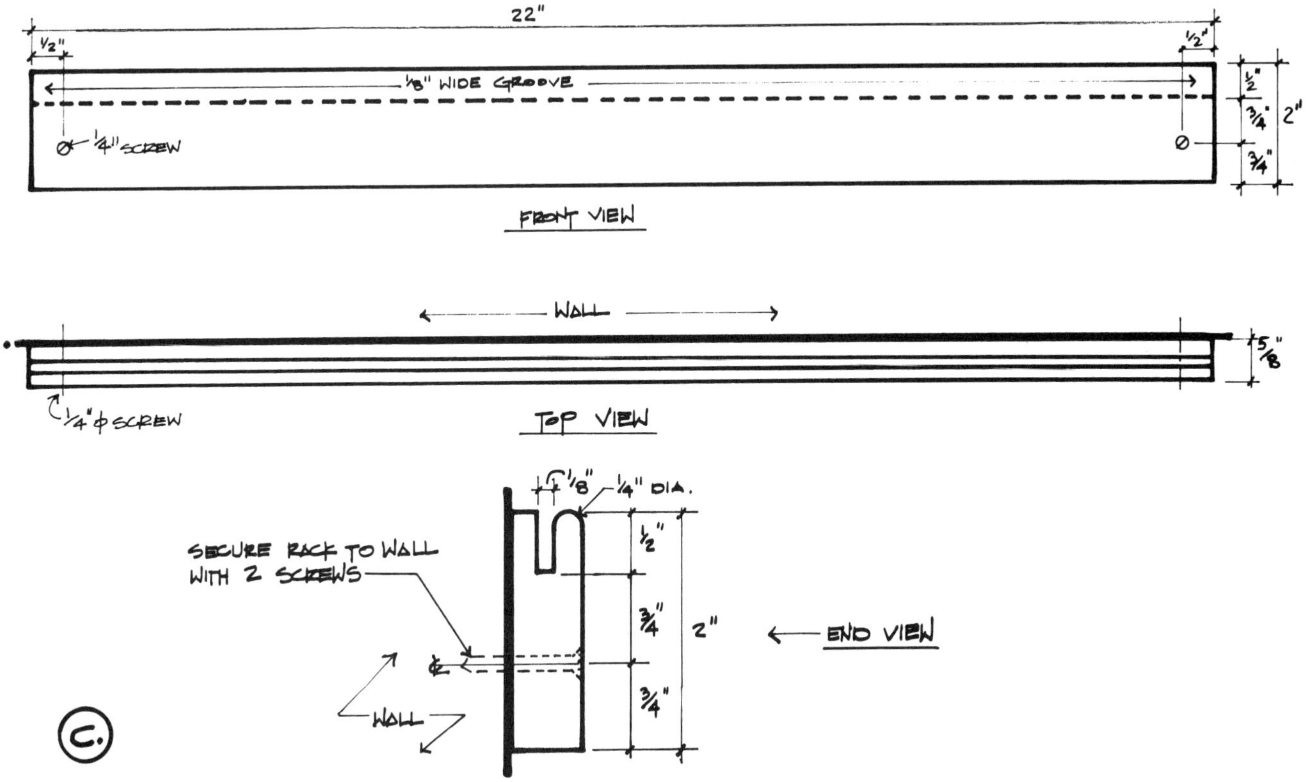
22"
1/2"
1/2"
1/8" WIDE GROOVE
1/4" SCREW
1/2"
3/4"
3/4"
2"
FRONT VIEW
WALL
5/8"
1/4" ϕ SCREW
TOP VIEW
1/8"
1/4" DIA.
SECURE RACK TO WALL WITH 2 SCREWS
1/2"
3/4"
3/4"
2"
WALL
END VIEW

C.

WALL-MOUNTED WINE GLASS RACK

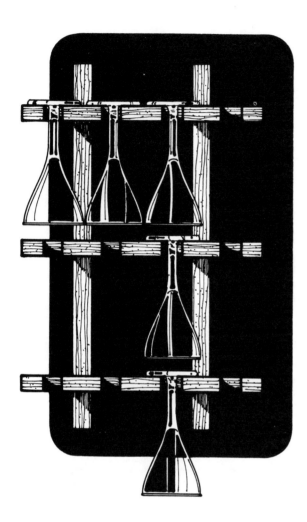

Glassware is another of those functional objects that have a great deal of visual appeal. It makes sense, therefore, to display your wine and other glasses for their decorative value, as well as for convenience, and what better way is there to show them off than with a handcrafted hardwood rack of your own making?

This version of the rack is a wall-mounted design with three cross members, each holding four glasses. It can easily be enlarged to display more items by adding to the length of each shelf or by adding more shelves, depending on the area you have with which to work. The placement of the slots and/or the distance between the shelves can be varied to accommodate your own glassware. Just be sure to allow enough room between slots, so that pieces can be hung and removed easily, without risk to neighboring glasses hanging on the rack.

WOOD AND OTHER MATERIALS

Choose a hardwood, such as oak, ash, or maple, that will complement its surroundings, as well as the glassware you plan to display. **Select three pieces that measure 4 by 12 by ¾ inch each and two pieces measuring 1 by 1 by 18 inches each.**

EQUIPMENT

Backsaw
¹⁄₁₆-inch and ½-inch drill bits, 1-inch circle attachment, and hand or power drill
Half-round file
Wood rasps 1 inch and ¾ inch
6 flathead wood screws, each ⅛ inch in diameter by 1¼ inches long
4 Molly bolts, each ¼ inch in diameter by 1½ inches long
Screwdriver
Sandpaper: grades 120, 220, 280, 400 (aluminum oxide paper)
Pencil #2
T-square
Mineral oil (or vegetable or olive oil)
Soft, lint-free cloth

PROCEDURE

Measure and cut the stock for the cross pieces and vertical supports. For the rack shown, three shelves and two supports are needed.

For each shelf, measure and mark the centers for the four holes that will be made for the slots, as indicated in Illustration A. Drill the holes, using the ½-inch drill bit and 1-inch circle attachment. To complete the slots, mark a line from the outside of each circle on the left and right to the front of the stock. Use a square to be sure all lines are parallel with the sides of the shelf. Cut in along each line to the predrilled hole. Once all slots are cut, smooth any irregularities with a half-round file.

Next, notch the back edge of each shelf where it will be attached to the vertical supports by measuring and marking the stock, as shown in Illustration B. Using a 1-inch wood rasp in an up-and-down motion, work inward to the required ¼-inch depth. Keep in mind that the width of the notch should be just slightly larger than the width of the vertical support that will fit into it. Too large a notch will mean a sloppy joint. The best way of ensuring a good fit is to compare the rasp to the support stock before making the notch.

When the cross members (shelves) are complete, proceed to notch the vertical supports, using the same method. Measure and mark the stock, and then use a ¾-inch rasp to make the notches. Again, double-check the notch width with the width of the shelf stock to assure a good fit.

Sand all pieces with coarse and progressing to fine sandpaper, giving special attention to the slots. To assemble the rack, drill a $\frac{1}{16}$-inch hole through the vertical supports at the center of each notch to accept the wood screws. Next, drill the same size hole into the center of each notch on the shelves to a depth of $\frac{1}{2}$ inch. To countersink the screws, enlarge the holes on the back side of the vertical supports using a drill bit which matches or is a little larger than the screw heads. Drill in just enough to accept the heads of the screws so that they will be flush with the surface. Sand off any burrs created by drilling.

Put the shelves in place and secure with the wood screws.

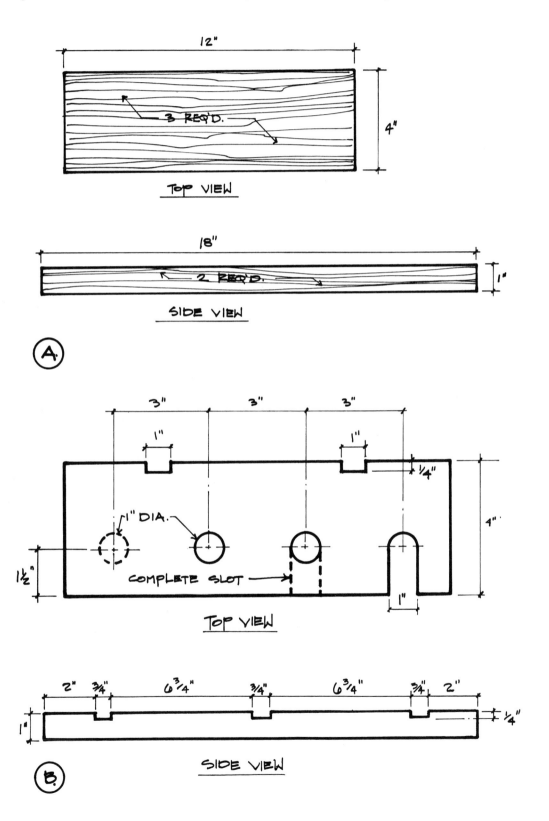

Establish the position of the hardware you will use to mount the rack on the wall. Drill holes for Molly bolts through the supports. Insert bolts after finishing.

The natural grain and color of the wood here will nicely complement the glassware it holds, and the interplay of glass and wood will be a pleasing accent wherever you hang your rack. Finish the wood simply by rubbing with mineral oil and buffing with a soft cloth. For a more permanent finish, you might consider varnish or lacquer, which dries to a hard, transparent film. (See finishing instructions in Chapter 3.)

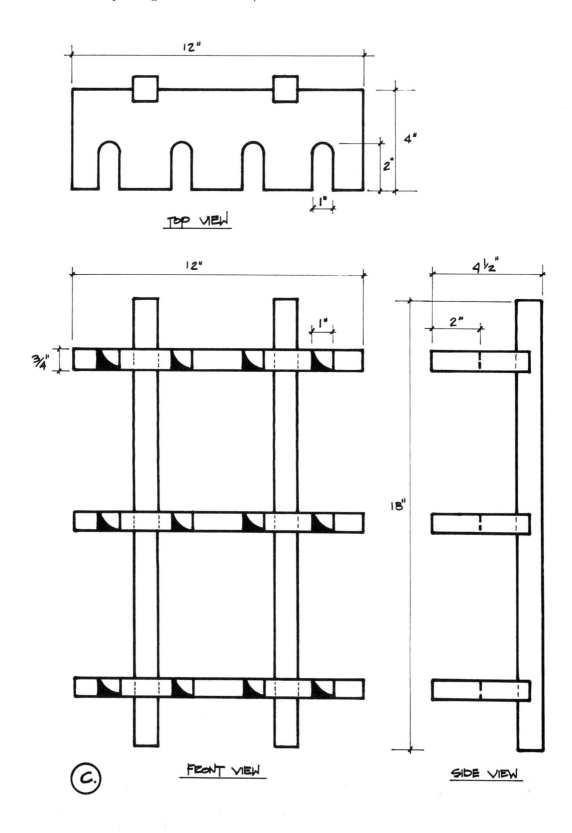

SUSPENDED WINE GLASS RACK

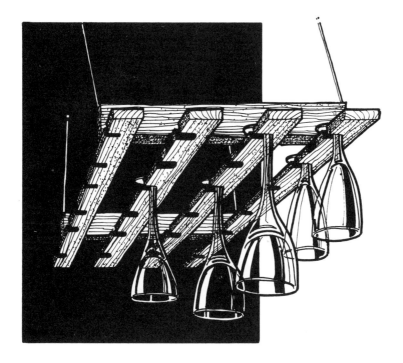

Easy access to the accoutrements of cooking and dining has always been a high priority of successful chefs and hosts. Not only is it practical to have things within reach, but it adds greatly to the flavor of the room to have the glow of wood, the shine of polished metal, and the glimmer of glass. This suspended wine glass rack not only serves these purposes, but provides extra storage space, a real bonus if shelf space is at a premium in your kitchen or dining area, as well. The rack can be altered to your own specifications—to accommodate more or less glassware or to accommodate pieces of different shapes and sizes. The illustrated version will hold twenty-four glasses and measures 24 by 28 inches overall.

WOOD AND OTHER MATERIALS

I recommend a hardwood, such as oak, beech, or maple, which will complement your decor and set off your glassware to the best advantage. **You will need four pieces, each 3 by 28 by 1 inch and two pieces, each 1 by 3 by 24 inches. You will also need 8 flathead wood screws, ⅛ inch in diameter by 1½ inches (brass screws, or wood filler to cover screws), 4 ring bolts ⅜ inch in diameter, 4 lengths of cable or chain for suspending rack, and 4 Molly bolts or other hardware for attachment to ceiling. Length of bolts should be no less than 2½ inches long.**

EQUIPMENT

Handsaw

$1/16$-inch, ⅛-inch, and ½-inch drill bits, 1-inch circle attachment, and hand or power drill

Screwdriver

Sandpaper: grades 120, 220, 280, 400 (aluminum oxide paper)

Pencil #2

T-square

Finishing materials of your choice

PROCEDURE

Cut all stock to size, as shown in Illustration A. To notch the cross pieces, measure and mark the centers of the 1-inch-diameter holes, which will be the interior portion of the slots. (See Illustration B.) Drill the 1-inch holes through the stock, using the ½-inch drill bit and the 1-inch circle attachment. Using a T-square, draw two parallel lines from the outer edges of each 1-inch hole to the front edge of the stock. Use a saw to cut in from the edge of the stock to the hole on each side, completing each slot.

When all slots are cut, sand all wood carefully, working from coarse to fine sandpaper. Smooth the interior surface of each slot, using a file, if necessary, to even out the juncture of saw cut and drilled hole before sanding.

Determine the placement of the screws on each cross piece, which will hold it to the supports. The screws should be centered between the outer two slots on each end and halfway between the front and back edges (1½ inches in from either edge). Mark these points, one on each end of each cross piece, and drill through the stock using the ¹⁄₁₆-inch drill bit.

Enlarge the top portion of each hole (on the face of the cross piece) to accept the head of the screw. You may want to countersink the screws below the surface of the wood and fill in the top of them with woodpaste for a pegged effect, or countersink just so that the screws are flush with the surface and leave them showing to accent the wood.

Brass-head screws would do well for this purpose.

Mark the 1- by 3-inch support pieces on one of the 1-inch faces to indicate the placement of the cross pieces as shown in Illustration C. To predrill the supports for assembly, mark a point at the center of the area, where the support will be joined to each cross piece (corresponding to the ¹⁄₁₆-inch holes already drilled in the four slotted pieces).

Assemble the rack by positioning the cross pieces on the supports and applying the wood screws. (If countersinking below the surface, fill in over screws with wood paste. Allow to dry and sand smooth.) Attach the ring bolts to the upper side of the supports by drilling to a depth of ½ inch, using a ⅛-inch drill bit and then turning the rings into the

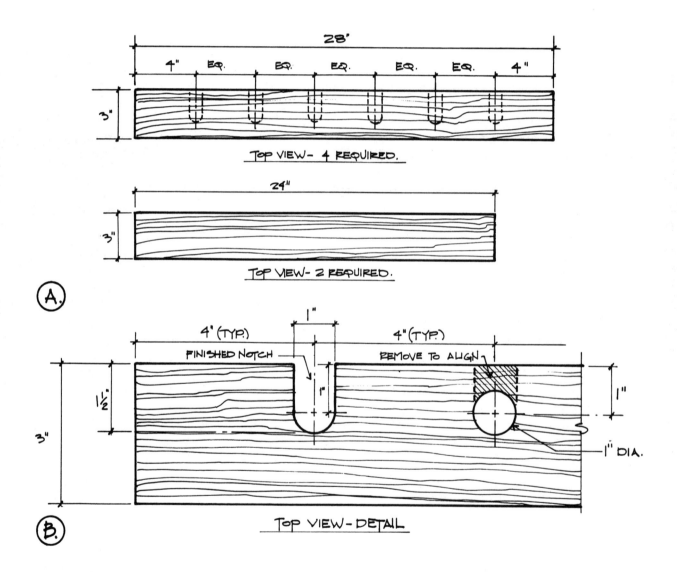

predrilled holes. The rings may be placed just above the other screws or at points centered halfway between the cross pieces on each side. After finishing the rack, hang it, using four lengths of cable or chain and Molly bolts positioned on the ceiling. (The length of the cable or chain will depend on your specific needs.)

Any finishing material of your choice may be used to complete the rack. Penetrating oil, varnish, or lacquer will give a permanent surface, which will stand up to long years of use. (See finishing section in Chapter 3 for procedure.)

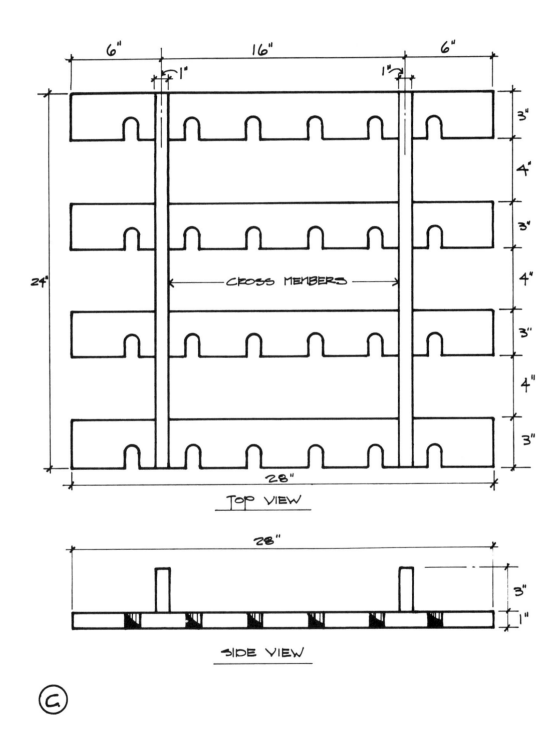

TOP VIEW

SIDE VIEW

WALL-MOUNTED KNIFE RACK

A set of strong, sharp, well-balanced kitchen knives are to the chef what fine surgical tools are to the surgeon. Top quality and efficient cutlery come in many sizes and shapes, each designed to carry out a specific function in the cook's hand. Often, however, knives are damaged as the result of abuse and not through misuse. Knives with wooden handles should never be placed in the dishwasher or thrown into the kitchen utensil drawer. Edges become knicked and dulled and the original fine hone must be professionally restored. Handles of larger cutlery tend to be nondescript. Therefore it is anyone's guess as to what the correct blade looks like when knives lay on top of one another in a plastic cutlery tray.

The solution to these annoyances is very simple. Make and use a wall-mounted knife rack that will: 1) put four to six knives in full view of the cook; 2) protect the sharp alignment of the cutting edge.

WOOD

Because the knife rack is subject to frequent use, it is suggested that a hardwood be used to withstand the rigors of kitchen duty. Maple, one of the hardest of woods, would make an excellent choice. Consider walnut or hickory for darker colors and relative hardness. Oak also offers an interesting possibility. **The two large pieces of wood measure 12 inches in length by 2 inches in height each. Spacers, of which two are needed, measure 2 inches high by ½ inch wide by ½ inch thick.**

EQUIPMENT

Backsaw
Waterproof white glue
2 C-clamps
¼-inch drill bit and hand or power drill
Screwdriver
Sandpaper grades: 120, 220, 280, 400 (aluminum oxide paper)
2 flathead wood screws, ¼ inch diameter
Pencil #2
Ruler

PROCEDURE

Begin by measuring out two 12- by 2- by ¼-inch pieces of wood. These will become the front and back plates of the knife rack. The rack requires two small spacers measuring ½ by ⅛ by 2 inches to be glued and clamped to the respective front and back plate as illustrated in Illustration B. Holes and screw sizes are given in Illustration B.

Once all four pieces have been cemented and allowed to dry, two holes are drilled, one on each end of the rack. The ¼-inch drill bit is used to make the two holes and should be made at the halfway mark of the board's height. A countersunk hole is more attractive to the front and should be considered in the final stages before the plate is flush-mounted to the kitchen wall.

If necessary, use 120 sandpaper to smooth over rough areas. Continue sanding with the finer grades. Finish with 400 aluminum oxide paper. No sealer is required. However, polyurethane finish will prolong the wood life. Food can be easily wiped away with a sponge provided the rack has been properly sanded and sealed.

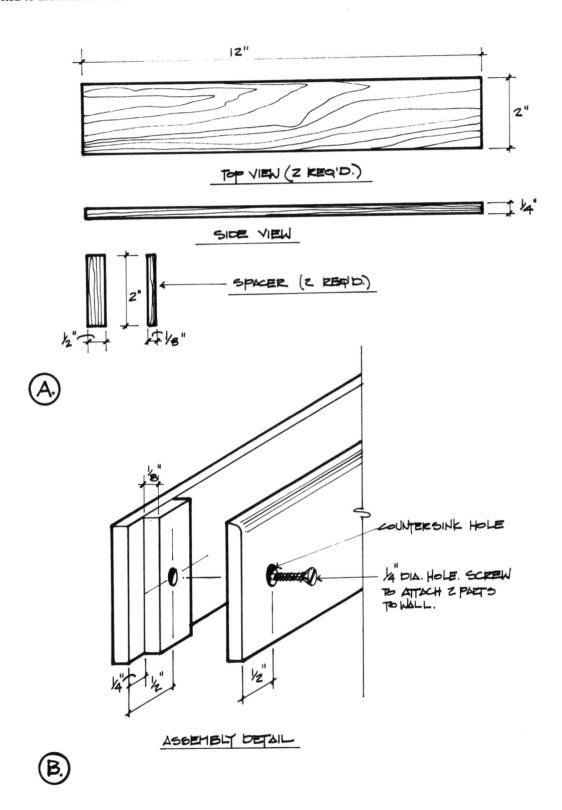

12"

2"

TOP VIEW (2 REQ'D.)

¼"

SIDE VIEW

SPACER (2 REQ'D.)

2"

½"   ⅛"

Ⓐ.

⅛"

COUNTERSINK HOLE

¼" DIA. HOLE. SCREW TO ATTACH 2 PARTS TO WALL.

¼"   ½"

½"

ASSEMBLY DETAIL

Ⓑ.

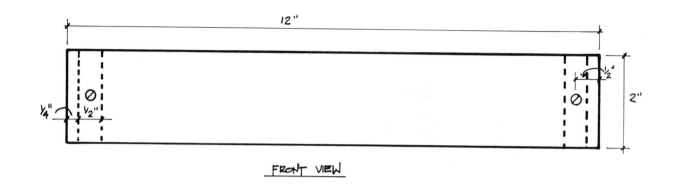

12"

2"

¼" ½" ½"

FRONT VIEW

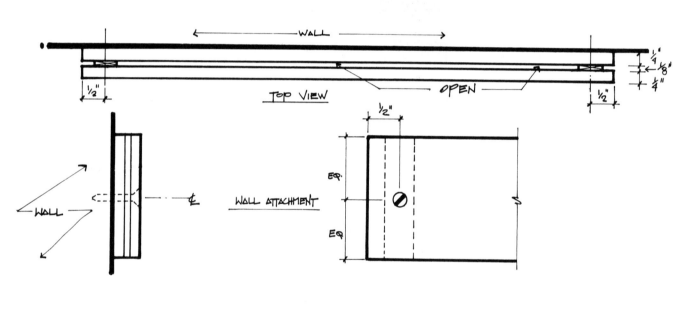

WALL

OPEN

TOP VIEW

½" ½" ¼" ⅛" ¼"

WALL

℄

WALL ATTACHMENT

½"

EQ.

EQ.

Ⓒ.

COUNTERTOP KNIFE RACK

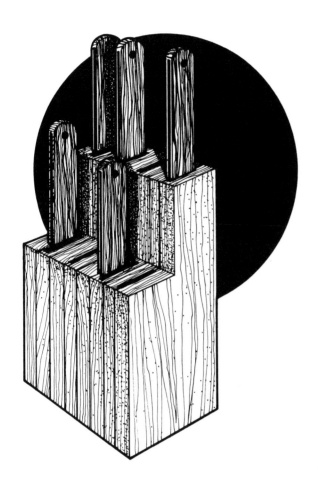

Sharp knives, whether used for eating or cutting of large meats, are often stored in drawers where they are easily dulled and even knicked. Too little circulation of air contributes to the warping of handles and occasionally the rusting of the rivet used to bind handle and blade. Good cutlery should be in the open, upright for quick use, and placed according to size, which is precisely what this rack serves to accomplish. There are no magnets to scratch the finely honed and buffed steel and all sharp edges are neatly tucked in its protective sheath.

WOOD

This is a project where just about any good-looking wood will do. I have made several of these racks from leftover pine strips and have discovered that despite the daily use and abuse each one takes, they last forever. Consider alternating the laminated woods with a light wood and dark wood for a refreshing contrast. Woods of the following dimensions are needed: **8 pieces measuring 18 by 8 by ¾ inch.** Note Illustration B for depiction of how each typical laminated unit interfaces.

EQUIPMENT
Handsaw
Wooden mallet
Flat wood chisel, 1 inch wide (must be very sharp)
Waterproof white glue
2 wood clamps
Sandpaper: grades 80, 120, 220
Pencil #2
Ruler

PROCEDURE
Dimension, mark, and saw all pieces of wood according to the sizes given in the illustration. Each interfacing strip is notched the full running length of the strip to accept the knife blade. The notch measures ⅛ inch in width and is cut in the following manner. With a handsaw, cut two lines to a depth of $1/16$ inch per strip of wood. With a flat chisel and mallet chisel, cut out thin slivers of wood to make a flat channel. With a flat wood file, smooth out the channel keeping all surfaces at right angles to one another. With a sandpaper block (sandpaper wrapped around a piece of wood) smooth out any remaining bumps.

Stack each block of wood one on top of another. A firm fit of interfacing pieces should result. Some sanding may be needed to remove an odd lump or slightly raised surface of the interfacing sides.

Next, apply a liberal amount of glue to both surfaces of each laminated portion of the rack, and, by means of your finger, spread the glue so that the entire surface is coated. With the two wood clamps on hand, assemble all parts, making sure that the bottom surface of the rack is absolutely flat. Clamp tightly without nippling the wood. The glue will ooze out of the joins, which should be quickly wiped off with a damp, lint-free rag.

Allow the clamped rack to stand overnight or for as long as the glue's directions indicate for best adhesion.

Remove clamps when the glue is dry and sand, beginning with the coarser grade of sandpaper and working through the finer grades.

If for some reason the bottom is not perfectly flat, use a flat wood file to obtain an even surface. Another alternative for this problem or just for an added touch, is to install a small rubber foot on each corner to raise the entire rack off the counter and to prevent slippage when knives are removed or replaced.

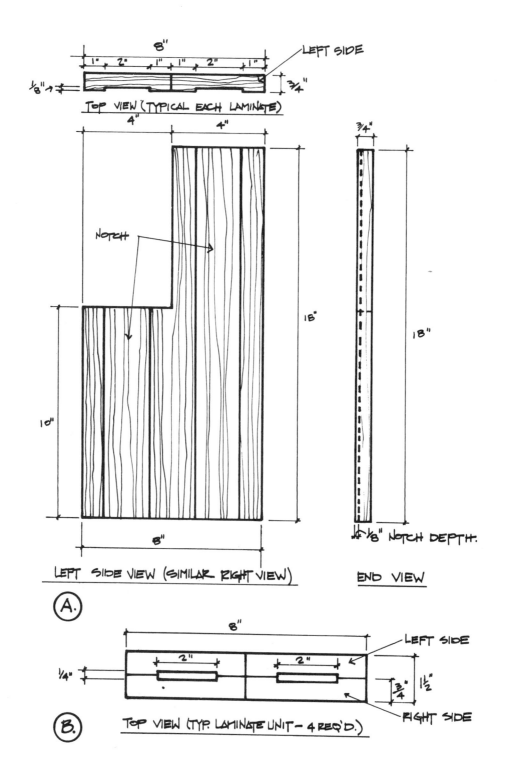

8"

1" 2" 1" 1" 2" 1"

LEFT SIDE

1/8"

3/4"

TOP VIEW (TYPICAL EACH LAMINATE)

4"   4"

NOTCH

18"

10"

3/4"

18"

8"

1/8" NOTCH DEPTH.

LEFT SIDE VIEW (SIMILAR RIGHT VIEW)

END VIEW

Ⓐ.

8"

LEFT SIDE

2"   2"

1/4"

3/4"   1 1/2"

RIGHT SIDE

Ⓑ.   TOP VIEW (TYP. LAMINATE UNIT - 4 REQ'D.)

116

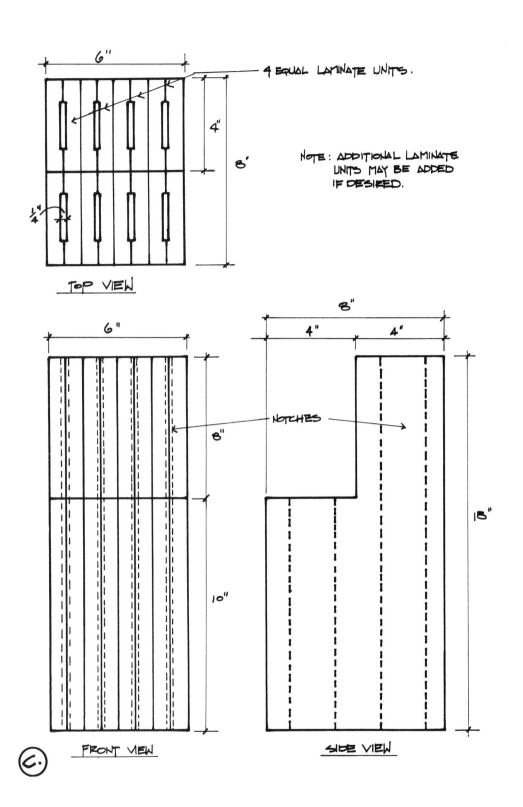

4 EQUAL LAMINATE UNITS.

NOTE: ADDITIONAL LAMINATE
UNITS MAY BE ADDED
IF DESIRED.

6"

4"

8'

$\frac{1}{4}$"

TOP VIEW

6"

8"

8"

10"

NOTCHES

8"

4"   4"

18"

FRONT VIEW

SIDE VIEW

C.

WINE BOTTLE RACK

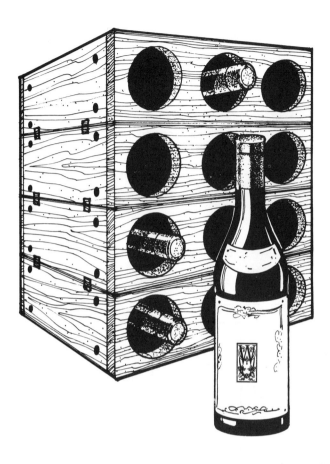

of the rails, which serve as supports for each row of bottles are also given. Six of these are needed. Also note at the bottom of Illustration A the drawing and size of blocking lumber. This is optional, but is to be encouraged to use for added strength. If you choose to side-step blocking, you will need to modify your measurements to better accommodate the rails.

A good hardwood, dark or light, is your best bet for strength. If cost is a factor, then investigate a good Douglas fir or even shop-grade plywood faced with a clear side. One-half inch plywood fits the bill nicely. Determine your overall square footage for each unit you plan to make and buy accordingly. The wine rack depicted in the illustration is composed of **four modules, each measuring 13½ by 5¼ by 12 inches. Front and back panel measure 13½ by 5¼ by ½ inch. You will need eight of these. Side panels, of which you will need eight also, measure 12 by 5¼ by ½ inch. Six rails measuring 13½ by ½ by ½ inch are required. Blocking, (optional) measures 4¼ by 1 by ¼ inch. Sixteen are required.**

You will also need thirty-two flathead woodscrews, each ¾ inch long and ½ inch in diameter.

EQUIPMENT
Electric radial saw or handsaw
Electric drill with ½-inch, ⅝-inch, and 3½-inch-diameter circle drill attachment
Wooden mallet
Flat wood chisel
2 adjustable wood clamps (must have the ability to clamp wood 14 inches or longer)
Try square
32 flathead wood screws, ¾ inch
Screwdriver
Sandpaper: grades 80, 120, 220
Carborundum paper: grades 400 and 600
Pencil #2
Ruler

PROCEDURE
With a ruler and pencil, dimension all pieces of wood according to the designated sizes and cut with a handsaw. If an electric radial saw is available, the cutting goes much faster. On each of the four front panels clearly mark the exact position of the circles to be cut as depicted in Illustration A. Cut the circles with the electric drill and circle attachment. Next, on each of the eight side panels, notch both top and bottom sides with the wood chisel and mallet. The notches are designed to accept the rails. Once notched, place the rails in position to check for fit. Some sanding with grade 80 sandpaper will ease the fit.

Illustration B shows where notches are to be made on both top and bottom panels. The channel of the notch

With the ever-increasing popularity of wine consumption and, in some cases, home wine-making, storage can present a problem. Wine is, of course, best preserved when allowed to rest on its side with an occasional rotation or two to keep sediment in a favorable mixture. A cool area of the kitchen or cellar is best for extended storage. It is precisely these concerns that make this design a winner for the woodworker faced with careful management of space in the home.

This wine rack is modular. One unit may be all that you need, but as the need arises, you may simply build another module, thus developing quite a storage rack for a more extensive collection. The plans for making the rack might look awfully involved to the uninitiated woodworker, but the unit is essentially just a box with twelve holes in it, not that different in shape or make-up from the cardboard or cheap wood crate from which the bottle originally came.

WOOD AND OTHER MATERIALS
To make this six-sided cube you will need sixteen panels cut to the dimensions indicated in Illustration A. The size

should be as straight as possible to ensure a smooth and correct alignment of the rails.

Predrill all pieces of wood where indicated with the electric drill and ½-inch drill bit. A second drilling with the ⅜-inch drill bit to a depth of ⅛ inch will permit the head of the screw to be countersunk or at least screwed flush to the surface of the wood.

Clamp the four sides of each level of the module and, with the screwdriver and ¾-inch long ½-inch-diameter screws, fasten all four sides. Repeat this procedure for the

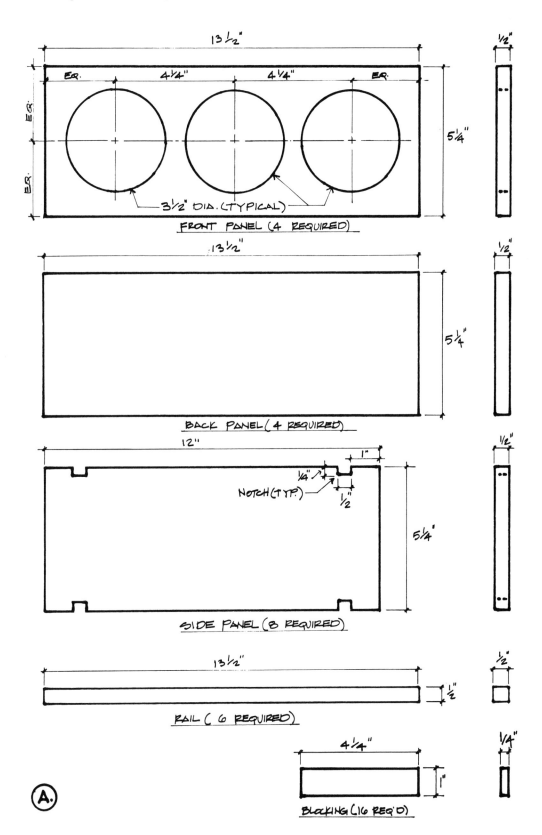

FRONT PANEL (4 REQUIRED)

BACK PANEL (4 REQUIRED)

SIDE PANEL (8 REQUIRED)

RAIL (6 REQUIRED)

BLOCKING (16 REQ'D)

(A.)

remaining three levels. If you intend to use blocking for additional strength, it now is installed along the inside right angle joints of the entire cube before the rails are fitted in the notches. A try square should be used to check the 90-degree alignment of all sides.

Install all rails by lightly tapping them into position with the mallet. The rails will give the rack even greater stability and rigidity where it counts.

Assemble the entire box one level at a time. Minor adjustments may need to be made as each level is fitted.

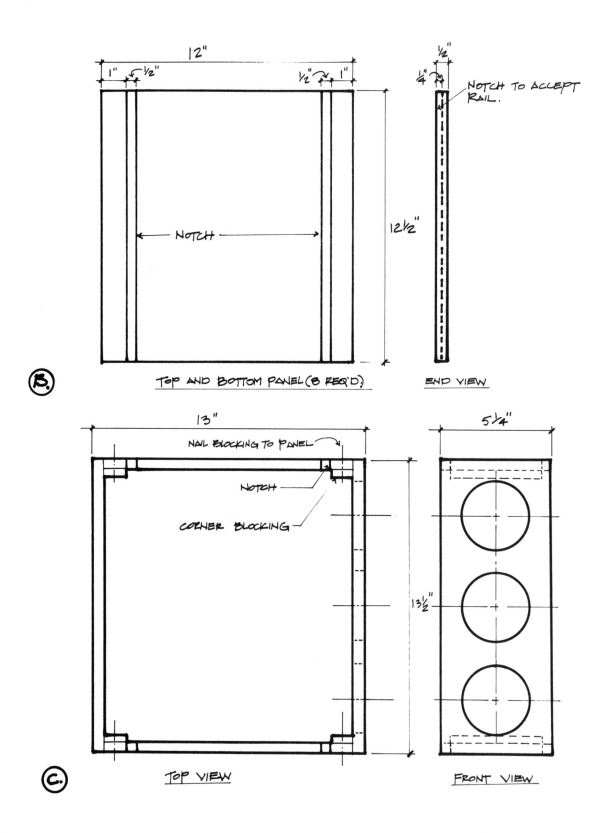

TOP AND BOTTOM PANEL (8 REQ'D.)

END VIEW

NOTCH TO ACCEPT RAIL.

NAIL BLOCKING TO PANEL

NOTCH

CORNER BLOCKING

TOP VIEW

FRONT VIEW

Again, sanding will usually remedy any slight binding that may have resulted from the sawing or notching steps.

Beginning with grade 80 sandpaper and moving up through the finer grades, sand the entire module. Finishing off with the carborundum papers. Sealing of the cube is optional.

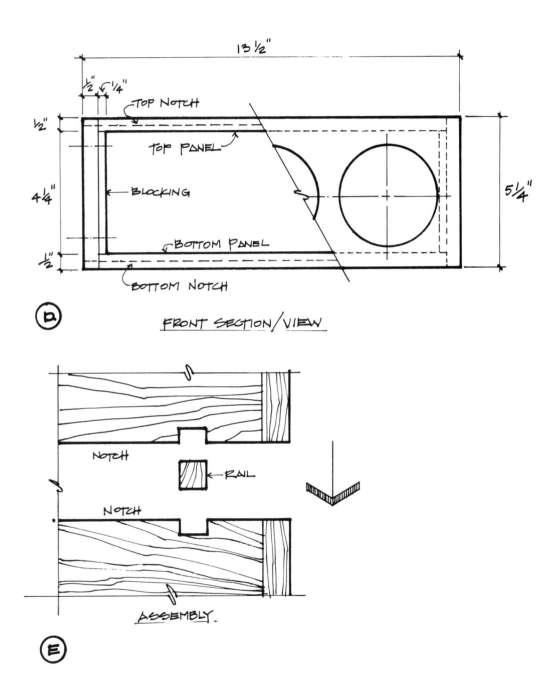

FRONT SECTION/VIEW

ASSEMBLY.

Glossary

Across the grain: at right angles to the direction of the grain of the wood.

Bevel: a sloped or slanted edge.

Bit: the part of the drill or brace which rotates and penetrates the wood. Often, interchangeable bits can be used with a given drill or brace.

Blanch: to cover with boiling water, drain, and rinse with cold water; a process used to remove skins or to bleach.

Burr: a rough edge, often produced when cutting or drilling.

Check: a lengthwise split or crack in the wood, often a result of the drying process.

Chuck: a part of a tool into which the bit is placed and secured.

Condiment: a seasoning, relish, or sauce used to add flavor to another food.

Countersink: to enlarge the top of a bored hole so that the head of the screw or nail will be flush with (or below) the surface of the wood.

Dice: to cut into small, usually cube-shaped pieces (used in preparing meats and vegetables).

Dimensioning: to cut or otherwise reduce wood to a required size. Also, to mark measurements on wood or paper.

Dowel: a round, wooden rod available in various lengths and diameters.

End grain: the cut end of a piece of lumber, showing the ends of the wood fibers.

Entree: the main dish (American usage), or the first course, consisting of a small portion of fish or other, served before the main dish (European usage).

Face: the principal surface of a piece of wood or the better-looking of two main surfaces.

Fold: to combine gently by turning two or more ingredients over from bottom to top without breaking air bubbles. Most often applied when adding whipped cream or beaten egg whites to other components.

Garnish: to decorate with something that adds color or flavor.

Heartwood: wood from the center core of the tree; often harder and sometimes of a different color than the outer layer of sapwood.

Inlay: a decorative technique, whereby pieces of contrasting wood or other material are set into the surface of the primary piece.

Julienne: food cut into long, thin strips, resembling matchsticks.

Kerf: the line or path made in the wood by the saw.

Macerate: to make soft or tender (to tenderize) by pounding or soaking.

Marinate: to soak food (usually meat or vegetables) in an acid or oil and acid mixture (such as lemon juice, wine, tomato, French dressing, etc.) to bring out flavor and tenderness. The soaking liquid is referred to as a "marinade."

Mince: to cut or chop into very small pieces.

Miter: a diagonal joint made by cutting two pieces of wood at 45-degree angles, so that when jointed, they form a right or 90-degree angle.

Relish: a highly seasoned food used as an accompaniment to other dishes to enhance flavor.

Sapwood: wood from the outermost part of the trunk, under the bark, which is often a different color than the inner core of heartwood.

Sauté: to cook quickly with a small amount of oil, turning and moving the food frequently.

Seasoned: a term applied to wood which has undergone a drying or curing process.

Shank: a thin piece of wood or metal usually packed into an area where two elements are joined to ensure a tight fit.

Sliver: to cut food (nuts, vegetables, or meat) into small bits or pieces, which are usually long and thin.

Springwood: that part of each growth ring produced in the spring or during wet periods when the tree grows most rapidly.

Stability: the ability of wood to retain its size, shape, and working properties after seasoning. A wood with low stability may absorb moisture in damp conditions and swell or distort.

Stock: the wood or lumber being used.

Strike: a short stroke with a hammer or mallet against a tool, such as a gouge or chisel.

Summerwood: the harder, denser part of each growth ring, produced in the summer or dry periods, when the tree grows more slowly.

Treen: small wooden objects or domestic items made of wood.

Whip: to stir vigorously, so as to beat air into the ingredients (cream, eggs, etc.) to produce a fluffy or stiff consistency.

With the grain: to work in the same direction as the grain of the wood.

Selected Bibliography

The following books are listed for the reader who wishes to find further information on topics covered in this book. They are grouped by subject and area interest. The majority of books that appear are still in print. Consult your local library or visit a secondhand book store and inquire as to the availability of hard-to-find titles.

EATING

Cassell's Vegetarian Cookery. London, Paris, and Melbourne: Cassell and Co., 1891.

Farmer, Fannie Merritt. *The Boston Cooking School Cook Book*. Boston: Little, Brown & Company, 1896.

Herman, Judith and Shalett, Marguerite. *The Cornucopia from 1390 to 1899*. New York: Harper & Row, Publishers, Inc., 1973.

Vasey, George. *Illustrations of Eating*. With a foreword by H. Richard Archer. Grant Dahlstrom, 1971.

Williams, W. Mattieu. *The Chemistry of Cookery*. D. Appleton & Co., 1885.

HAND AND POWER TOOLS

Daniels, George. *How to Use Hand and Power Tools*. New York: Barnes & Noble Books, 1964.

Jackson, Albert and Day, David. *Tools and How to Use Them*. New York: Alfred A. Knopf, Inc., 1978.

Salaman, R. A. *Dictionary of Tools Used in the Woodworking & Allied Trades c. 1700-1970*. New York: Charles Scribner's Sons, 1976.

Schuler, Stanley. *The Illustrated Encyclopedia of Carpentry and Woodworking Tools, Terms and Materials*. Chester, Conn.: Pequot Press, 1973.

KITCHENWARE

Conran, Terence. *The Kitchen Book*. New York: Crown Publishers, Inc., 1977.

The Cook's Catalogue. Introduction by James Beard. New York: Harper & Row, Publishers, Inc. 1975.

Deacon, Richard. *Microwave Cookery*. Tucson, Ariz.: H.P. Books, 1977.

Gould, Mary Earle. *Early American Wooden Ware*. Rutland, Vt.: Charles E. Tuttle Co., Inc., 1962.

The International Cook's Catalogue. Introduction by James Beard. New York: Random House, Inc., 1977.

Japanese Spoons and Ladles. Introduction by Yoshio Akioka. Tokyo: Kodansha International, 1979.

Lantz, Louise. *Old American Kitchenware*. Nashville, Tenn.: Thomas Nelson, Inc., 1974.

Objects for Preparing Food. New York: The Museum of Contemporary Crafts, 1972.

Shea, John G. *Making Authentic Shaker Furniture*. New York: Dover, 1992.

Steinberg, Rafael. *The Cooking of Japan*. Alexandria, Va.: Time-Life Books, Inc., 1969.

WOOD

Design and Aesthetics in Wood. State University of New York, 1972.

Edlin, Herbert. *What Wood Is That?* New York: The Viking Press, 1977.

The International Book of Wood. New York: Simon & Schuster, Inc., 1976.

Schiffer, Nancy and Herbert. *Woods We Live With*. Schiffer Limited, 1977.

WOOD FINISHING

Gibbia, S. W. *Wood: Finishing and Refinishing*. New York: Van Nostrand Reinhold Company, 1971.

Wood, Metal, and Plastic. Edited by Saul Lapidus. New York: David McKay Co., Inc., 1978.

Weights, Measures, and Cooking Conversion Table

The four basic metric measures are: meters (for lengths), liters (for liquids), grams (for solids), and degrees Centigrade (for temperatures)

METRIC AND IMPERIAL MEASURES

1 meter is about **3 feet 3 inches**
10 centimeters are about **4 inches**
1 centimeter is about **$2/5$ inch**
1 millimeter is about **$1/25$ inch**
28 grams is about **1 ounce**
1 kilogram is about **2 pounds**
1 liter equals **1¾ pints**
½ liter equals **18 fluid ounces** equals about **½ pint**
10 square centimeter equals **1 square inch**

To Convert	Multiply	By
ounces to grams	ounces	28.35
grams to ounces	grams	0.035
liters to British quarts	liters	0.88
liters to American quarts	liters	0.95
British quarts to liters	quarts	1.14
American quarts to liters	quarts	1.057
inches to centimeters	inches	2.54
centimeters to inches	centimeters	0.39

United States, British and Metric Recipe Equivalents

Ingredient	U.S.	British	Metric
Flour	1 tbsp	¼ oz	10 g
	4 tbsp	1 oz	25 g
	8 tbsp	2 oz	50 g
	¼ cup	1 oz	25 g
	½ cup	3 oz	75 g
	$2/3$ cup	4 oz	125 g
	1 cup	5 oz	150 g
Sugar	4 tbsp	2 oz. castor su.	50 g
	8 tbsp	¼ lb	125 g
	¼ cup	2 oz	50 g
	½ cup	3 oz	75 g
	$2/3$ cup	4 oz	125 g
	1 cup	7 oz	200 g
liquids	¼ cup	2 fl oz	0.0568 liter
	½ cup	4 fl oz	0.125 liter
	$2/3$ cup	5 fl oz	0.143 liter
	¾ cup	6 fl oz	0.166 liter
	1 cup	8 fl oz	0.25 liter
	2 cups	16 fl oz	0.5 liter

Index